Books by Jurgen Kuczynski

THREE HUNDRED MILLION SLAVES AND SERFS

ECONOMICS OF BARBARISM (WITH M. WITT)

HUNGER AND WORK

LABOUR CONDITIONS IN WESTERN EUROPE

NEW FASHIONS IN WAGE THEORY

GERMANY: ECONOMIC AND LABOR
CONDITIONS UNDER FASCISM

LABOUR CONDITIONS IN GREAT BRITAIN

1750 TO THE PRESENT

LABOUR CONDITIONS
IN GREAT BRITAIN

1750 TO THE PRESENT

BY JURGEN KUCZYNSKI

INTERNATIONAL PUBLISHERS, NEW YORK

PRINTED IN U.S.A.

To

THE MEMBERS OF THE
ACADEMY OF SCIENCES OF THE U.S.S.R.
WHO SET AN EXAMPLE TO THE
SCIENTISTS OF ALL OTHER COUNTRIES
BY THEIR DETERMINED FIGHT AGAINST
REACTION AND BY THEIR DEVOTED
SERVICE TO PROGRESS

"In every civilization of the past, bar none, . . . (there) was always a lousy standard of living."

MILO PERKINS, *Surplus Marketing Administrator, U.S. Department of Agriculture.*

CONTENTS

PREFACE TO THE SECOND EDITION

IN 1942 I published *A Short History of Labour Conditions in Great Britain and the Empire*, and within less than one year the edition was sold out. The book bristles with statistics, contains an unusually large number of tables, and is by no means easy reading. Why, then, was the book in demand?

The reason no doubt is that the subject is arousing more and more interest, and that those who want to study it have few books from which to choose. Moreover, in the course of discussions with persons in many different walks of life, I have found that the book does at least possess the merit of raising problems that have been passed over in silence by most writers on labour conditions.

But I have found, too, that I made the mistake of regarding certain facts as well established and generally accepted. Many things that I should have done to explain in more detail were left with little explanation or none.

In these circumstances the most satisfactory course would perhaps have been to rewrite some parts of the book. But the delay in publication would have been considerable, and printing conditions in war time would have added further difficulties. So I have left the text practically unchanged, adding instead a new lengthy introduction.

This, however, has not been enough. For, while I was engaged in writing two further volumes of this *Short History of Labour Conditions* my attention was fixed upon certain interesting problems to which I had given inadequate consideration in my study of Britain and the British Empire. Then, again, during the last year or two, students of labour conditions have made considerable progress in the specific field of the worker's health. These several matters I have dealt with both in the new introduction and in additional chapters.

Finally, statistical information, although still deplorably scanty, has been increasing of late, so that it is now possible to give a more detailed survey of the development of labour conditions during the present war. I have accordingly added a special chapter on the state of labour conditions since 1939.

Taking Great Britain alone into consideration, these additions have almost doubled the length of my original manuscript. The book, if printed in one volume, would now be too costly, its price putting it beyond the reach of most workers. This edition will therefore appear in two volumes, the first dealing with Great Britain, the second—which will come out shortly—with the Empire.

In conclusion I wish to express my thanks to my publisher, Mr. Frederick Muller, for his helpfulness during the whole course of our transactions. He it is who in these difficult times has made it possible for this *Short History of Labour Conditions* to appear. And in providing the paper for this second edition while new volumes are with the printer or in preparation, he has gone beyond that which any writer could hope for.

J. KUCZYNSKI

LONDON,
May 1st, 1944.

INTRODUCTION TO THE SECOND EDITION

THE chief contention in this book is that labour conditions under industrial capitalism have deteriorated absolutely as well as relatively. In this introduction I shall endeavour to show how this has come about, to describe the various intricate processes by which the standard of living of the workers has—in spite of many contrary appearances—worsened, and to explain how under capitalism there can be only seeming exceptions to this general law.

There are many persons who will not accept the evidence for absolute deterioration nor the theory. For some of these objectors the mere fact that Marx has developed the theory is enough to make them reject it. Others—and it is surprising to find so learned a critic as Leonard Woolf among them—reject the evidence because it does not confirm hazy impressions and reminiscences of youthful days. At any rate, no better grounds are mentioned by Mr. Woolf when he says: "If one considers contemporary accounts of such conditions in autobiographies, biographies, historical and sociological works, or novels, the evidence, it seems to me, is of a marked improvement in general conditions of life. The evidence of one's own memory points in the same direction. It extends in my own case to fifty years of life in London and south coast villages. It seems to me incontestable that the standard of living of the London worker and of the Sussex agricultural labourer, bad though it is to-day, is considerably better than it was in 1893."*

And if we turn to the working class we find many sincere students of social conditions who, although profoundly dissatisfied with the existing state of affairs, and firm in the conviction that economic injustice and waste are inseparably connected with the capitalist system, yet believe that they are better off than their parents and grand-parents. As one worker asked, after having read my volume on the United States: "But isn't a worker with a Ford better off than one without a Ford?"

* *The New Statesman and Nation*, January 23, 1943.

It is in an endeavour to help to clear away such confusions of mind and doubts that I shall now try to give a brief explanation of the theory of absolute deterioration as developed by Marx and to answer in some detail the question, whether a worker with a Ford is not better off than a worker without one.

1. THE THEORY OF ABSOLUTE DETERIORATION

The rejection of the theory of absolute deterioration is something fairly new. In the early years of capitalism it was regarded as natural or as ordained by God that the poor should be poor, and even that with the growth of wealth the poor should grow in number and their misery increase. Ortes, one of the finest and most clearly thinking clerical economists in the eighteenth century, builds his explanation for the need of Christian virtues largely upon the fact that so much misery does and must exist in this world. The Rev. J. Townsend speaks of hunger as "not only a peaceable, silent, unremitted pressure, but as the most natural motive to industry and labour, it calls forth the most powerful exertions." And from this he concludes that the continued existence of hungry people is a blessing to mankind. "It seems to be a law of nature that the poor should be to a certain degree improvident" (Marx remarks when quoting this: "so improvident as to be born without a silver spoon in the mouth") "that there may always be some to fulfil the most servile, the most sordid, and the most ignoble offices in the community."*

Destutt de Tracy refines this theory further by showing that Townsend's "law of nature" not only makes the poor improvident, but makes the people who are improvident enough to live in capitalist countries poor: "In poor nations the people are comfortable; it is the rich nations where they are generally poor."† The theory of the dynamic growth of poverty, regarding misery not as a static gift of nature or God, but as a fine product of society is well expressed by Storch‡: "The progress of social wealth begets this useful class of society . . . which performs the

---

* Quoted in *Capital*, vol. i, chap. 25. The pamphlet by Townsend is called *A Dissertation on the Poor Laws*, and Townsend uses the *nom de plume* "A Well-Wisher of Mankind."

† *Traité de la Volonté et de ses Effets*, Paris, 1826, p. 231.

‡ *Cours de l'Economie Politique*, St. Petersburg, 1815, vol. iii, p. 223.

most wearisome, the vilest, the most disgusting functions, which takes, in a word, on its shoulders all that is disagreeable and servile in life, and procures thus for other classes leisure, serenity of mind and conventional* dignity of character."

While these men do not deny the extent of misery and openly declare that it grows with the increase of wealth†, the first indications of a certain uneasiness make their appearance almost at the same time. They are expressed in statements which imply that the poverty is not only natural but really also a source of pleasure. I have quoted in the text of this volume‡ comments by Archdeacon Paley on the almost orgiastic pleasure experienced by the poor man when he succeeds in making both ends meet— a pleasure denied to the rich man who has so much money that he cannot taste the sweetness of "ends just meeting." It is interesting to note that recently a similar line has been taken up by ultra-reactionaries in this country who want to preserve for the poor the pleasure of free competition for jobs under conditions of unemployment and the happiness derived through actually succeeding for some time to keep a job. But it must be conceded that the finest expression of this spirit comes from the pen of an American business man :§

"Only those permitted to labour industriously and who know how to abound in honest poverty can be free, contented and secure. Poverty is a bulwark of liberty, a guarantee of tranquillity of spirit and a safeguard from danger."

But with the growth of a labour bureaucracy, with the spread of opportunism in the labour movement, with the emergence of a "social conscience" in the bourgeoisie combined with a fear of changes in society, the notion that there must always be poor people, and that their conditions must not improve if national wealth is to grow, has become less widespread, less "popular." The old dicta on capitalist society have been exchanged for new ones which promise labour a better future—an improvement

* "*C'est bon!*" exclaimed Marx when quoting him. *Capital*, vol. i, chap. 25.
† Just as the great state theorists from Bodin to Rousseau, Adam Smith and Kant never denied that one of the chief tasks of the state was the protection of private property.
‡ See pp. 49–50.
§ H. Drane, *The Dallas Morning News*, quoted in *New Republic*, June 7, 1943.

guaranteed by the alleged improvement which has taken place in the past. And this denial of the theory of absolute deterioration and of the evidence in its favour has steadily increased in vigour as labour has gradually come to realize the true connection between poverty and capitalism.

*   *   *

There is one decisive difference between the early, naïve theories of absolute deterioration and the theory as developed by Marx: Marx shows how the capitalist system creates—and proves that it must create—conditions under which the lot of the worker deteriorates. I am going to try to explain in a few words the fundamental principles of this theory while leaving a more detailed description to the last volume of this *Short History of Labour Conditions*. There I shall deal with the general laws of the development and the methodology of studying labour conditions.

The Marxist theory of absolute deterioration states two things: firstly, that under capitalism the size of the proletariat tends to increase, and secondly, that the working and living conditions of the proletariat tend to deteriorate. The growth of misery, therefore, is a twofold one: the number of people affected is increasing, and the degree of misery is growing.

Nobody denies even to-day when so many fundamental truths are being denied that with the growth of capitalism the size of the proletariat tends to increase. The growth of industry, the absorption of an increasing part of the population in capitalist production through the growth of the factory system, the relative decline of the number of people with a small business of their own are facts upon which there is no disagreement. "Accumulation of capital is, therefore, increase of the proletariat," says Marx.*

But why, though the size of the proletariat is increasing, is their misery increasing too? The first reason, of course, is that the employers tend to pay the workers as little as possible in order to increase their profits as much as possible. As Marx says, commenting upon the statement by John Stuart Mill that "if labour could be had without purchase, wages might be dispensed with,"†

---

* *Capital*, vol. i, chap. 25.
† *Essays on Some Unsettled Questions of Political Economy*, London, 1849, p. 90.

"But if the labourers could live on air they could not be bought at any price. The zero of their cost is therefore a limit in a mathematical sense, always beyond reach, although we can always approximate more and more nearly to it. The constant tendency of capital is to force the cost of labour back towards this zero."*

While there is general agreement on the fact that the size of the proletariat tends to increase, there are already a number of people who would deny that the capitalists have the tendency to pay as little as possible. However, their number is not very great, especially in the labour movement, and probably one can say that, generally speaking, there is at least some sort of agreement on these points.

The question now arises: Why, under capitalism, are the employers able to get the better of labour, even when labour is organized? Many persons who are prepared to admit that employers like to reduce wages to the lowest possible figure, stoutly maintain that Labour is strong enough to prevent Capital from having its way.† Marx explains this inherent weakness of Labour's position as follows:

"Simultaneously with the progress of accumulation there takes place a progressive change in the composition of capital. That part of the aggregate capital which consists of fixed capital, machinery, raw materials, means of production in all possible forms, progressively increases as compared with the other part of capital, which is laid out in wages or in the purchase of labour. . . . . In the progress of industry the demand for labour keeps, therefore, no pace with the accumulation of capital. It will still increase, but increase in a constantly diminishing ratio as compared with the increase of capital."‡

That means, there is a tendency for productivity per worker to increase more quickly than production. In this case workers are thrown out of work and what Marx calls "an industrial reserve army" is created.

Now both tendencies, the tendency for capital to grow quickly

* L.c. chap. 24.
† See, for instance, also an otherwise as staunch a defender of Marx against bourgeois economist theories as Paul M. Sweezy, *The Theory of Capitalist Development*, p. 19.
‡ *Value, Price and Profit*, last chapter.

and to attract an ever greater number of workers, and the tendency for the composition of capital to change so as to release labour, to make it superfluous, to create an army of unemployed, are to be observed working side by side. A technical improvement, the introduction of machines into a new field of production, at first throws workers on the street, productivity increases faster than production, an army of unemployed is created. After a while the demand for the new and cheaper product rises rapidly, production increases more than productivity per worker has increased, and there is renewed demand for labour; the number of workers employed in this industry or branch of industry rises.* Marx has shown in Chapter XXV of Volume I of *Capital* the various modifications which this process undergoes under varying conditions, how some factors intensify it while others tend to slow it down. But whatever the particular conditions, capital not only tends to create, but actually does create, a reserve army which on the one hand enables it suddenly to expand production, and on the other hand, decisively weakens labour's fighting strength. The existence of a pool of unemployed makes the economic struggle a very unequal one. The workers cannot, as did the bourgeoisie or the feudal ruling class, gain economic power and establish a mode of production of their own (socialism) as a step towards gaining political power. As Marx says:†

"The law, finally, that always equilibrates the relative surplus-population, or industrial reserve army, to the extent and energy

---

* Marx describes the often simultaneous realization of these tendencies in chap. 25, vol. i: "Considering the social capital in its totality, the movement of its accumulation now causes periodical changes, affecting it more or less as a whole, now distributes its various phases simultaneously over the different spheres of production. In some spheres a change in the composition of capital occurs without increase of its absolute magnitude, as a consequence of simple centralization; in others the absolute growth of capital is connected with absolute diminution of its variable constituent or of the labour power absorbed by it; in others again, capital continues growing for a time on its given technical basis, and attracts additional labour-power in proportion to its increase, while at other times it undergoes organic change, and lessens its variable constituent; in all spheres, the increase of the variable part of capital, and therefore of the number of labourers employed by it, is always connected with violent fluctuations and transitory production of surplus-population, whether this takes the more striking form of the repulsion of labourers already employed, or the less evident but not less real form of the more difficult absorption of the additional labouring population through the usual channels."

† *Capital*, vol. i, chap. 25.

of accumulation, this law rivets the labourer to capital more firmly than the wedges of Vulcan did Prometheus to the rock. It establishes an accumulation of misery, corresponding with accumulation of capital. Accumulation of wealth at one pole is, therefore, at the same time accumulation of misery, agony of toil, slavery, ignorance, brutality, mental degradation, at the opposite pole, i.e., on the side of the class that produces its own product in the form of capital." And: "It follows, therefore, that in proportion as capital accumulates, the lot of the labourer, be his payment high or low, must grow worse."

"In proportion as capital accumulates, the lot of the labourer must grow worse"—that is the law of the absolute deterioration of labour conditions—for in the proportion as capital accumulates the industrial reserve army grows and labour gets weaker in its bargaining position, and the growth of labour organizations while preparing the way for political victory can only impede but not stop the decline of the economic strength of labour.

Marx leaves not the slightest doubt about this inherent weakness of labour within the framework of the capitalist system. He says, for instance, in *Value, Price and Profit*, last chapter: ". . . the working class ought not to exaggerate to themselves the ultimate working of these everyday struggles. They ought not to forget that they are fighting with effects; that they are retarding the downward movement, but not changing its direction; that they are applying palliatives, not curing the malady. They ought, therefore, not to be exclusively absorbed in these unavoidable guerrilla fights incessantly springing up from the never-ceasing encroachments of capital or changes of the market."

The theory of the absolute deterioration of labour was probably the first fundamental theory worked out by Marx. Early in his study of economics he concentrated on this phenomenon of capitalist society and worked out its implications. I have quoted extensively from *Capital*, published in 1867, and from *Value, Price and Profit* written in 1865. I will conclude my brief exposition of his theory with a quotation from the economic-philosophical manuscripts he wrote in 1844, at the age of twenty-six, almost a quarter of a century before the publication of the first volume of *Capital*:

"The worker becomes the poorer, the more wealth he produces, the more his production increases in power and size. The worker becomes an ever cheaper commodity the more commodities he produces. The more valuable use is made of the world of objects, the greater the devaluation of the world of the human being."*

*   *   *

2. SOME PRACTICAL QUESTIONS AND ANSWERS REGARDING THE PRESENT STATE OF LABOUR

The deterioration of labour conditions, although certain, is not a simple process the evidence for which is easily to be picked out from the continually changing aspects of our social life. It cannot be substantiated by any series of clearly-cut statements of fact regarding any one of the elements forming the whole pattern of the workers' life. For instance, it cannot be truly stated that real wages are continuously declining. Nor that the working day is constantly lengthening. Nor that the intensity of work is unbrokenly increasing. Nor that the health of the workers continues year by year to grow worse. Nor that accidents are everywhere and in all recent years more numerous than they were fifty years ago, and still more numerous than they were a hundred years ago. The matter is not as simple as that. It cannot even be maintained that the conditions of any special group of workers —miners or carpenters, weavers or agricultural labourers—are deteriorating steadily, year by year. Nor can this be said of the conditions of the whole working class in any one country. Nay, it may even be found that the conditions of the workers in some one country have improved somewhat over a particular trade-cycle—perhaps even over two. But what cannot be asserted is that under the capitalist system the conditions of all workers employed by one country's capital have improved from one trade-cycle to another. That is, it may happen that, for a short time, labour conditions, e.g. in the United States improve—but one

* *Gesamtausgabe, Erste Abteilung*, vol. iii. The original German reads as follows: "Der Arbeiter wird umso ärmer, je mehr Reichtum er produziert, je mehr seine Produktion an Macht und Umfang zunimmt. Der Arbeiter wird eine umso wohlfeilere Ware, je mehr Waren er schafft. Mit der Verwertung der Sachenwelt nimmt die Entwertung der Menschenwelt in direktem Verhältnis zu."

will find then, that conditions of people exploited and plundered by American capitalism in other countries deteriorate rapidly and that conditions of all people under the domination of American capital, inside and outside the U.S.A., continue to deteriorate.

It is because the deterioration of the conditions of the workers takes place in such varied ways that it requires such careful study. It takes place in ways that vary with the varied history of capitalism in the different countries of the world. To give a comprehensive picture of it is almost impossible, if only for the reason that the study of this subject has been neglected for more than half a century, and that consequently the necessary data are often not to be found. And, finally, of course, the deterioration of labour conditions is camouflaged to an enormous degree by any advance in our complex civilization. The worker enjoys certain real as well as seeming improvements in his surroundings. So that the task of making a true evaluation of all these changes in terms of real amelioration or deterioration in his lot becomes exceedingly complex.

Those who want to believe that, although conditions are not all they ought to be, they are improving on the whole, rest with complacency upon the complexity of the subject. They do not welcome an attempt to disentangle the truth from the deceptive appearances that hide it. In his already mentioned review of this volume Leonard Woolf writes:

"Mr. Kuczynski shows his lack of scientific objectivity in two ways. The first* is accumulative; whatever the betting, the ball always falls into the red hole. If money wages show an increase, real wages, which have to be based upon a considerable amount of calculation and often approximate or weighted figures†, almost always cancel this out and show a decrease. If real wages persist in showing an increase, Mr. Kuczynski will show that they

* Mr. Woolf's second argument I have already mentioned; it is that I do not rely on the memory either of Mr. Woolf or others about the improvements of conditions but rather prefer statistical evidence—not so surprising in a statistical study which uses other evidence only when the statistical evidence is either not available or not adequate.

† This, although Mr. Woolf does not realize it, is a stab at those highly respectable bourgeois statisticians, whose cost of living computations I have used. One of them being in the employ of one of the leading Wall Street journals; it is improbable that they computed cost of living figures favouring the theory of absolute deterioration.

really deteriorated owing to increased intensity of work.* If the death rate of children under ten years declines, the statistics, he maintains, tell us nothing about the state of health of these children,† and are therefore no evidence of improvement in conditions of life; but an increase in the death rate does tell us something about the children's health and is evidence of deterioration of conditions, because 'it is extremely improbable that the state of health improves while the death rate increases.' "

This criticism of Mr. Woolf's indicates that I have not failed entirely in indicating the various ways in which labour conditions can and do deteriorate, nor in showing how—and that is the decisive point—"the ball always falls into the red hole."

But it does not always fall for all workers into "the red hole." There is no doubt that for some groups of workers labour conditions have improved over a lengthy period—to mention the most important one: the labour aristocracy. There are some groups of workers who live under capitalist working conditions and yet are well off—for instance, the small number of highly skilled diamond cutters. Almost all workers are better off in years of increasing trade activity than in periods of depression and crisis. A change in the distribution of industry over a country may bring a definite improvement on a local scale—for instance for day labourers in a predominantly agricultural district which becomes an armament centre. The whole working class of a country may benefit temporarily—even from one trade cycle to another—if the capitalists of this country are able at the same time to increase their profits from special exploitation of newly acquired countries or spheres of interest. It is possible, for instance, that the workers in the United States were better off from 1915 to 1929 than during the preceding fifteen years because of the special exploitation facilities the American capitalists had in other American and Allied countries during the war—and in Europe and other American countries after the war. But all these are no arguments against the fact that the conditions of the workers employed by the capitalists of a given country have been and are, on the whole, deteriorating.

* I do, of course, not show that real wages have "really deteriorated," but explain that increased intensity of work requires increased intake of food and increased rest.

† See on this point p. 23 of this introduction.

And now to come to the question whether a worker. with a Ford is not better off than one without a Ford. It is only a partial answer to point out that sometimes the Ford eats more and better than the worker who owns it. That is to say that a worker with a Ford has to forego sufficient food in order to be able to keep a car and thus travel to and from his place of work which cannot be reached by bus, tram or other public vehicle.

Engels, too, has come across such a question. In his study on *The Housing Question*, Part I, he writes:

"The English proletarian of 1872 is on an infinitely higher level than the rural weaver of 1772 with his 'hearth and home.' Will the troglodyte with his cave, the Australian aborigine with his clay hut, and the Indian with his hearth ever accomplish a June insurrection and a Paris Commune?"

How, then can Engels speak of an absolute deterioration of the conditions of the workers if he maintains that the level to-day is a higher one than that of a hundred years ago, and incomparably higher than that of the cave-dwellers? He can not only do this, but he does so, and in the very next sentence:

"That the situation of the workers has in general become materially worse since the introduction of capitalist production on a large scale is doubted only by the bourgeoisie.* But should we, therefore, look backward longingly to the (likewise very meagre) flesh-pots of Egypt, to rural small-scale industry, which produced only servile souls, or to 'the savages?' On the contrary."

Well, in what, then, does the deterioration of the conditions of the worker consist? In what respects is a British worker of to-day worse off than his forefathers at the beginning of the industrial revolution? When he sits down to his meal to-day his more civilized surroundings usually give him the appearance of enjoying a higher standard of life than was theirs of the eighteenth century. His room will very likely be lighted by electricity, his crockery will be less rough and crude, his chair will at any rate look more comfortable, his kitchen utensils may in some respects be more convenient. He may be able to listen to the wireless

* This is the only statement by Marx or Engels on the theory of absolute deterioration which Leonard Woolf has proved to be wrong (though unfortunately he is not even original in this and by no means the first member of the Labour Party to doubt the validity of the theory of absolute deterioration!)

during his meal; a newspaper may be at his elbow (in 1750 even a weekly paper was an unheard-of luxury).

All this, unfortunately, although not without importance, is negligible compared with another point. And upon this vital point it is possible to speak both accurately and emphatically. The following table needs to be studied with care for it is truly eloquent.

THE DIET OF A WORKER*

Nutrient	Diet of English Labourer Eighteenth Century	Diet of over 15 Million People in 1935	Modern Estimate of Requirements
Calcium (grms.)	1·2	0·5	1·0
Iron (mgrms.)	23	9·6	15
Vitamin A (International Units)	6,600	1,220	5,000
Vitamin B1 (International Units)	1,300	350	500–700
Vitamin C (mgrms.) ..	110	55	75

It is hardly necessary to point out that of all man's needs nutrition comes first. What a man eats largely determines whether it is possible for him to be healthy in body and mind. And it is an indisputable fact that the British worker to-day, although enjoying a higher cultural standard, and occupying a rather more comfortable (although not necessarily healthier) home, actually lives on a lower nutritional level than did his forefathers of two hundred years ago.

But does that mean that we want to go back to the eighteenth century with its relatively primitive standards of living? or even further back to the cave-dweller whose diet from a nutritional point of view may perhaps have been even better than that of the English worker in the eighteenth century? Of course not! But we are against going back to the eighteenth century not because we are against sufficient nutrition. We do not want to go back because we want to go forward to a life where the higher cultural standard of to-day is combined with food as sufficiently nourishing as that of the past, and even better.

* Quoted from Sir John Boyd Orr, *Food and the People*, London, 1943, p. 15. The figures for the eighteenth century were computed by Professor Drummond; the figures for 1935 refer to families spending less than 9s. per head per week on food; Orr says that they are more than one-third of the population. The modern estimate of requirements is given by Orr in the same book.

A similar surprise as the above table on nutrition is in store for those who study health conditions. It is well-known that the death rate has declined considerably during this period. The expectation of life of an English labourer in the eighteenth century was about 30 years. In 1935 it was about double that figure. This improvement is due partly to better sanitary conditions, and partly to a more widespread use of medical science. But does this mean that the health of the worker is better to-day than two hundred years ago? Does this mean that the worker is healthier while he is alive than he was two hundred years ago? No such assumption can be made. While in a period of progressing medical science and the increasing application of its results we may assume that an increase in the death rate means a deterioration in health conditions, we are not justified in assuming that every decline of the death rate means an improvement of health. Let us listen to Sir John Orr on this subject :* "As a result of this deterioration in the nutritional value of the diet of the working classes, the physique of the people deteriorated. . . . The average stature fell. . . . This deterioration in the nutritional state and physique of the people was masked by the reduction in the death-rate which followed the elimination of epidemic and endemic diseases, such as cholera, enteric and typhus fever, through the application of modern sanitary principles." Again we ask : do we want to return to the life of one hundred and two hundred years ago when epidemics were rampant, sanitary conditions on a very low level, when medical science had progressed far less than to-day, but when the people—as far as they survived—were of better physique and health? Of course not! But there is just as little doubt that we not only want the better state of health and physique of two hundred years ago but want a still healthier and stronger people, able to enjoy the cultural progress made during the last two centuries, and the greater progress yet in store for them.

These facts alone justify us in stating that there has been a deterioration of labour conditions. For if the worker is worse fed, if his state of health is inferior, then his energies are less and

---

* Quoted from Sir John Boyd Orr, *Food and the People*, London, 1943, p. 15.

more easily exhausted; and thus his standard of living has declined. It does not mean, however, that his cultural standard, his moral standard, as Marx once called it, has declined.

Clearly we have to distinguish between the primitive necessities of life such as food, adequate clothing and warmth in winter, and other factors which contribute to a man's well-being without being in themselves necessities. And in this connection one further explanation must be made. It is no part of the theory of absolute deterioration that under capitalism all necessities of life become scarcer for all groups of workers all the time. It may well happen that for some workers during some periods there will be a rise in the standard of living in many respects. It may well happen also that there is an absolute improvement in respect of some necessities for all workers over a long period. But this improvement will always be found to be more than counterbalanced by some deterioration elsewhere. Or, perhaps the rise will show itself upon closer examination to be deceptive. For instance, there is no doubt that sleep is one of the absolute necessities of life. And there is equally little doubt that the worker can sleep to-day longer than one hundred years ago because his working day is shorter. But it must be remembered that the amount of sleep a man requires varies with his output of energy during the day. Increased intensity of work makes it necessary for him to have a longer period for rest and recuperation. Thus, it may well be that a man enjoying to-day 20 per cent more sleep than his great grandfather of one hundred years ago is nevertheless in a worse case. And the same may be true of an improved diet, the need for which must be measured not in absolute terms but in requirements of an increasingly exhausted body. Similarly, an improved standard of housing may be paid for at the expense of a lowered standard of feeding or vice versa.*

I have said enough, I hope, to show that the study of standards of living is a very complex one. The reader of this volume and of the others in the series will find numerous illustrations of the fact that deterioration takes place not only with considerable variations in time, place and group affected, but also with considerable variations in the kind and method of deterioration. But whatever the country's particular process of development

* See this volume, p. 108.

may have been, the fundamental law of absolute deterioration of labour conditions under capitalism is always exemplified.

3. The Theory of the Relative Deterioration of Labour Conditions

The theory of the relative deterioration of labour conditions has also been developed by Marx. In one of his earliest studies of labour problems, *Wage-Labour and Capital*, he gives considerable weight to the problem of relative wages, that is wages expressing the relative position of the worker's standard of living as compared with that of the capitalist's. At the end of Chapter VI of this study he writes: "Wages are determined above all by their relation to the gain, the profit, of the capitalist. In other words, wages are a proportionate, relative quantity." And again: "Real wages express the price of labour power in relation to the price of other commodities; relative wages, on the other hand, express the share of immediate labour in the value newly created by it, in relation to the share of it which falls to accumulated labour, to capital."

Why do labour conditions deteriorate relatively? Why does a declining share of the national product go to labour? Or, in other words why does the individual worker get a constantly declining and the capitalist a constantly increasing share in the national product? There are various ways of explaining this, the simplest being a corollary of the theory of absolute deterioration. If national wealth increases, if the worker's position become absolutely worse, and if through increased accumulation of capital in the hands of the individual capitalists the position of the individual capitalist improves absolutely, then it is obvious that the condition of the worker must deteriorate in relation to that of the capitalist.

Not until the beginning of the twentieth century were there many men who disputed the fact that the relative position of the worker was deteriorating. But with the spread of a social conscience in the bourgeoisie as a whole* in the last few decades,

* I do not mean the courageous and honourable activities of progressive men in the bourgeoisie since over one hundred years, nor do I mean the sincere sympathy shown for the poor by humanitarians, but the "social conscience" as a political and sociological conception.

it has become customary to deny that the abyss between the rich and the poor has grown. Complaints about death duties are mingled with attempts to prove that wealth is being more equally distributed among the people; and the hysterical outcry against the "process of socialisation" which is alleged to be well under way, is mixed with propaganda asserting that if the distribution of wealth is no longer equitable this is due to the fact that the rich have to give away too much.

I have worked out some figures on the development of relative wages in Britain and the United States, and these clearly show the extent of the relative deterioration of labour conditions, the extent of the extraordinary decline of relative wages.* But I want to give here some additional data which are of particular interest because they throw light on one aspect of the conditions of the rich and the poor which is studied much too little: their relative death rate. It is true that the death rate among children of all classes has decreased greatly during the present century, and this is not the place to analyse in detail the causes of this improvement. But it is especially interesting to investigate an aspect of relative labour conditions where an absolute improvement is registered. The following figures are taken from the masterly investigations by Dr. Titmuss into birth, poverty and wealth.†

INFANT MORTALITY BY CLASS OF FATHER
(100 Average Rate for All Classes)

Class	1911	1930–32
Middle and Upper Classes ..	61	53
Low-paid Workers	122	125

While the death rate itself has declined for all classes, the difference between the mortality among the children of the rich and among the children of the poor has grown considerably. But this is only the beginning of the study by Dr. Titmuss. He proceeds to investigate the causes of the deaths. Children of course die partly for reasons not directly, or not at all, connected with the social status of their parents, especially so in the first days and weeks after birth. Dr. Titmuss has, therefore, made

* See p. 119 of this book, and p. 172, vol. ii.
† *Birth, Poverty and Wealth*, London, 1943.

a special investigation into the mortality of children by age and cause of death. The next table, however, does not take yet directly into account the various causes for death and refers only to the death rate by age groups:

PERCENTAGE EXCESS OF INFANT MORTALITY OF THE CHIL DREN OF THE LOW-PAID WORKERS OVER THOSE OF THE MIDDLE AND UPPER CLASSES, 1911 TO 1932

Age of Children	1911	1921–23	1930–32
0 to 1 month	106	58	66
1 to 3 months	180	263	239
3 to 6 months	253	312	330
6 to 12 months	299	324	498

This table shows that with increasing age, that is with an increasing share of environmental diseases as the cause of death, the excess of mortality among the poor over that of the rich rises, and that in the older age groups the excess was relatively higher in 1921–1923 than in 1911, and relatively higher again in 1930–1932 than in 1921–23.

While it is impossible to get at equally reliable figures linking age with the kind of disease which caused death for the three periods, it is possible to make some investigation for 1930–1932, and to connect these figures with some data available for 1921–1923. The result of this investigation is expressed as follows:*

"When we turn to the group of environmental diseases, death rooted in bad housing, nutritional deficiencies, defective clothing, ignorance, inadequate medical care and a host of attendant evils, then we see in full measure the gulf that divides one social class from another; the privileged from the under-privileged. What is no less striking than the extent of the difference is the fact that the gap increased after 1921–1923 and, for all we know, may still be growing."

This is a remarkable sidelight on the problem of the relative deterioration of the position of the worker. In a small but highly important and sorely neglected field of social statistics the relative deterioration of the position of the worker finds a striking expression. It is true that these figures do not prove that there is an all-round relative deterioration—for there might theoretically be other and on the whole more important aspects of the situation

* *Birth, Poverty and Wealth*, London, 1943, p. 51.

showing a contrary tendency—but these figures, if taken together with more general data given later in this book, are a useful and impressive rejoinder to all those who have not only no "belief" in the theory and history of the absolute deterioration of labour conditions, but do their best to persuade the people that the rich are getting poorer and the poor are getting richer—until in the very near future the rich have become poor and the poor rich, and we must start again at the beginning.

I would like to end these remarks on the relative deterioration of labour conditions by saying that while it would be wrong to concentrate on the study of its theory and practice, that while the problems of absolute deterioration are infinitely more important—that ought to be no reason to continue to neglect it, especially as far as its statistical measurement is concerned. Dr. Titmuss has done magnificent work in his special field,* but there are so many other aspects in the life of the worker which ought to be scrutinized from this point of view that an enormous task remains to be done.

*   *   *

These few remarks have given but a partial description of the theories of absolute and relative deterioration, and they have been even less adequate as an indication of the implications of the two theories. I shall deal with these matters more fully in the last volume of this series. But I hope that they will suffice as a first introduction to the theory and as a useful start for the perusal of the following history, which is a history of "the practical working out" of these theories.

---

* Cf. on this specific subject also the valuable study by G. H. Daniel, "Social and Economic Conditions and the Incidence of Rheumatic Heart Disease," *Journal of the Royal Statistical Society*, Part III, 1942, and the most recent study by J. N. Morris and R. M. Titmuss on "Recent History of Rheumatic Heart Disease," *The Medical Officer*, 1944.

PREFACE AND INTRODUCTION

ALL who belong to the masses of wage-earning and salaried workers, and all who study carefully the working and living conditions of these masses are agreed that labour conditions are bad. They are not always bad for all sections of the working class; there are exceptions, and such exceptions may embrace considerable parts of the working class at one time or another. But whether we study Engels' writings a hundred years ago, or those of Charles Booth and Seebohm Rowntree at the end of the last and the beginning of the present century, or those of Sir John Orr to-day—we find them all agreed that there is much misery among the toiling masses of this country. Such misery, however, is not only to be found in Great Britain and the Empire. It is to be found almost everywhere, at any time during the last one hundred and fifty years.

Among those who have studied the problem of labour conditions, and also among those who have suffered from hunger and misery and oppression, there have been two groups, each with a different programme of change. The one group believes in slow reform within the capitalist system; they are called and often call themselves reformers or reformists. The other believes that only a radical change of society and relations within society, only the abolition of the system of capitalism, in fact, can bring about a change in the conditions of labour; they are called and call themselves socialists.

The reformers and reformists are not blind believers in sudden progress under capitalism. They are not mystics. They base their belief on the lesson of history as they interpret it. They are of the opinion that labour conditions in general and the standard of living of the working class have improved under capitalism and that they will continue to do so under sufficient pressure from the trade unions and the political parties—operating within the framework of the capitalist system.

The socialists, too, refer to history. In addition they have worked out a theoretical system, scientific socialism, which, they believe, gives not only a theoretical basis for and an explanation of the past experience of history but which also proves that future experience under capitalism will inevitably be the same as that of the past. An improvement in the standard of living of the working class will not be possible within the capitalist system; it will be possible only after the abolition of the capitalist system and its replacement by socialism.

Both groups have produced a great many studies of labour conditions—the most famous ones have been written by socialists. These studies deal with separate phases or separate aspects of the history of labour conditions under industrial capitalism.

In the present volume I try to give a connected history of labour conditions, and of the standard of living of the workers in Great Britain and in the Empire* since the beginning of "industrial capitalism," that is since the introduction of the factory system up to the present day. It is the first volume of a short but comprehensive history of world labour conditions under industrial capitalism. The second volume will deal with labour conditions in the United States, the third with Germany, the fourth with France, and so on. I hope to be able to round off this history with a seventh volume dealing with theoretical and methodological problems.†

In this book, then, I have tried to gather together the most important evidence at our disposal (statistical in character and chiefly that published under official auspices) concerning the development of labour conditions and of the standard of living of the working class. Furthermore, I have tried not only to assemble all the relevant facts: after they have been put together I have tried to evaluate their importance, and to arrive at conclusions as to the actual course of development. In other words, I have attempted to come to conclusions as to whether labour conditions and the standard of living of the working class have improved or deteriorated; if so why; and whether they

---

* Eire, which has shown so much independence politically and economically, has been left out of consideration—but, of course, not Ireland under British rule.

† I have dealt briefly with such problems in my *Labour Conditions in Western Europe 1820 to 1935*.

have changed for the working class as a whole or only for parts of it.

*   *   *

It is important, before proceeding further, to give an explanation of what is understood in this and in the following volumes by "labour conditions" and "standard of living" of the working class.

Some people may say: this is an extremely simple problem. If, for instance, the workers can buy more and better food and clothing, or can rent better furnished rooms (electricity instead of gas, etc.) because of increased purchasing power, then obviously the standard of living has improved. And since not a single person who understands anything of this subject can deny that the purchasing power of the workers has increased during the last hundred and fifty years, this book is superfluous if it seeks merely to investigate whether the standard of living of the workers has improved or not, since, let us say, 1790. Only those books which deal with the problem of the extent to which the standard of living has improved deal with a really worthwhile problem in this view.

This is a clear-cut and simple point of view, the validity of which, however, can easily be shaken by a single question. Some time ago the British Press printed the news that the German miners in the Ruhr-territory get vitamin tablets, a measure which undoubtedly improves their standard of nutrition. But does this mean that the German miners' standard of living has really improved? No—it simply means that the German miners are better nourished in order to enable them to stand the constantly increased pace of production. Better nourishment does not, necessarily, mean better working and living conditions.

Thus, we see clearly that those who base their evaluation of conditions, and measure the increase in the standard of living solely by the increase of real wages, that is of the purchasing power of the workers, receive and give a wrong picture of what actually happens to the worker, to his standard of living and to labour conditions.

It will be one of the tasks of this study to present the whole of labour conditions, the whole of the factors affecting the standard of living, and to strike a balance between the various factors tending to improve and to deteriorate this standard, to strike a balance, for instance, between increased real wages and shortened hours of work on the one hand and increased intensity of work on the other, between increased security through a system of social legislation and greater insecurity through increased and more widespread unemployment, between better safety legislation and the installation of accident preventing devices on the one hand and greater speed-up and greater fatigue tending to increase the rate of accidents on the other.

Apart from these elements in the standard of living of the people there is another which Marx calls the moral element, which is an expression of the general progress of society and methods of production. A better knowledge of medicine and the fear of epidemics has led to an improvement in general sanitary conditions. The complicated technique of industrial production, the introduction of machinery requiring skill and knowledge from the workers, has led to the introduction of a general system of education. Here, we undoubtedly have a certain progress; the moral element in the standard of living, that element connected with the general progress of society has certainly grown. But here again various questions of importance arise. Has the worker unrestricted facilities to learn and study all he wants? Or is he allowed to learn only what the progress of industrial technique requires him to learn? Is the worker free to study even though he is economically unfree? Improved sanitary conditions have undoubtedly much contributed to lower the death rate. But is he free to enjoy his prolonged life? Is the worker free to enjoy his prolonged life when he has to work for his living under conditions which are not interrelated with the progress medicine has made? While the moral element in his standard of living has grown in importance, has it grown only as much as is needed in order to make the worker work more or to make him a lesser danger (in the event of epidemics) to those for whom he has to work?

*   *   *

The reader of the first volume will realize at once that a seven-volume history of labour conditions under industrial capitalism is inadequate. There is no doubt that a detailed history of labour conditions in Britain and in the British Empire, for instance, cannot be written in a volume less than four times the size of this book, without failing to deal with a considerable number of important problems. On the other hand, a world history of labour conditions is urgently needed, and I cannot see much hope of one being written and completed in the near future if a start were made with a long and detailed survey of Britain and the British Empire.

Limitations of scope and of space have had serious consequences for the presentation of this material: Some problems are dealt with only fleetingly because other studies dealing with them are available. This applies particularly to the history of the trade union and political labour movement. In Britain, in France, in Germany, and in the United States a number of books have been published dealing with the history of the labour movement in these countries. True, the subject has not been dealt with adequately for any of these countries, but the available studies are sufficient to give a background knowledge. Other problems are dealt with only in one or two volumes of the present study. For example, the interesting problem of the influence upon wages and employment of free or relatively free land settlement, which could actually be dealt with in a review of conditions in Australia, will be treated only in the volume on the United States. The same holds true of the history of some trade union theories on wages and hours of work. On the other hand, the influence of gold discoveries upon the living standard of the people will be dealt with only summarily in the volume on the United States, but the chapter dealing with labour conditions in Australia will consider it in more detail. Again, the important fact that employers have begun to re-apply methods of exploitation in use during the early period of industrial capitalism (lengthening of the working day, lowering of real wages, etc.) will be dealt with quite briefly in most of the volumes, but will be considered in greatest detail in the case of Germany, where Fascism has outstripped other countries in the application of both cruder and subtler methods of exploitation. The present volume devotes, of course, special attention to labour conditions in the Dominions and Colonies, and the volume on France will deal also with other aspects of these problems.

My treatment of the subject of labour conditions is statistical. That is, wherever possible I have tried to give figures which reveal the course of development of the various aspects of labour conditions. And when no figures were available I have given only few indications of what occurred. That is, these volumes deal chiefly with problems which can be presented statistically, and I have indicated other aspects of labour conditions only in order to round off the picture without dealing with them in great detail. This necessarily means a narrowing of the field covered by this series of studies.*

Finally, the field is still further narrowed by the fact that I deal chiefly with conditions of labour directly working under industrial and, in later phases, under finance capitalism, or imperialism. For example, while only touching upon the conditions of the agricultural population in India, I give more detailed statistics of the conditions of industrial labour and of plantation labour.

To all these voluntary restrictions in the field of investigation are added a great number of unavoidable restrictions, arising out of the paucity of our information on many subjects.

In spite of all these shortcomings and voluntary restrictions, I hope, nevertheless, that a clear enough picture is presented of each of the countries dealt with to indicate the general trend of the development of labour conditions, and at the same time to give some idea also of the peculiarities of labour conditions in the different countries.

I hope, too, that I have added to our statistical knowledge and to the existing statistical methods of measuring labour conditions. Sometimes that was easy. Incredible though it may sound, and in spite of the fact that the statistical material is readily available to anybody interested in the subject, this book is the first to contain, among other things, an index of wages for Australia since 1850. Considerably more difficult was the construction of a wage index for India, and this must not be regarded as more than a first approximation. The index of unproductivity, drawn up for the first time for Great Britain, is, I

---

* For this reason, with the exception of India, the present "colonial part" of the Empire is not dealt with in this book, except for some Notes at the end of the book on "Food and Health in the Colonial Empire."

think, an improvement upon my index of unproductivity in the United States published in a former study of mine.* The statistical study of the relative position of labour has not made much progress since I published my first statistics fifteen years ago, and the figures given in this volume do not go much beyond those given in former works of mine.

* * *

Before concluding this introductory preface I want to say a few words about statistics and politics. While statisticians of every political colour have expressed complete agreement with my statistical technique they have often reproved me for using my statistical knowledge for political purposes. This was perhaps most amusingly expressed in a review of my book *Hunger and Work* in *The Economist*, where the following was said:

"The defects of this book are less of technique than of deliberate and avowed bias. 'La statistique est une mâitresse perfide qui égare ses adorateurs' (Statistics is a mistress who makes fools of her admirers), someone once said. But Mr. Kuczynski is no ardent seeker after truth led astray by a too uncritical reliance on his statistics. To continue the metaphor, he is no Don José seduced and deceived by a fickle mistress. On the contrary, he has coldly exploited her for his own ends, those ends which he explains in the preface:

"'The book is written to put into the hands of the workers computations based on Government material, which will help them in their fight for higher wages, to assist trade unionists in negotiations for better living conditions . . . for all those who . . . are ready to fight for the general welfare of the people and for social justice.'"

My answer to *The Economist* is:

I shall always make use of my statistical knowledge in the interest of the people. I shall always endeavour to do it in such a way that the technique is faultless, that the training I have got has not been misspent. I hope that I shall succeed more and

* *New Fashions in Wage Theory.*

more in presenting just those statistics which the working class and the people as a whole need in their fight for freedom and democracy. If that is bias then I hope I shall get more and more "biassed."

JÜRGEN KUCZYNSKI

LONDON,
February 23rd, 1942.

CHAPTER I

1750 TO 1850

"WHEN Queen Anne came to the throne the long struggle for
the supremacy of the seas which we had waged with varying
success since the pioneer days of Drake and Hawkins was nearly
over. The once great power of Portugal and Spain was little
more than a memory. The French were badly crippled after
the treaty of Utrecht in 1713. The Dutch were being out-
manœuvred and outrivalled on every trade route. Everywhere
overseas our merchants were in the ascendancy; at home our
industries were developing rapidly. For the first fifty years of
the century fortune smiled on most of the people of England."*

Indeed, the ruling classes of Britain, foremost among them
the agricultural capitalists, but no less so the commercial
capitalists, could be well satisfied with the world in the first half
of the eighteenth century.

Conditions among the masses of the people were bad. But
they did not go from bad to worse. On the contrary, it is not
improbable that they tended to improve a little. Harvests were
good, prices of food remained relatively stable, unemployment
tended to decline rather than to increase. It is true, the small
tenant farmers suffered severely; it is true that in the south-
western regions of England conditions for the masses of the
people probably tended to deteriorate; but, taking Britain as a
whole, one is justified in saying that for the masses of the people
there had rarely been a period during which conditions showed
fewer tendencies towards worsening and more towards improving.

All this changed rapidly with the turn of the half century and
even more so as the end of the century approached. The period
beginning with 1750 and ending with 1850, that is, the years
immediately preceding the "industrial revolution," and the

* J. C. Drummond and Anne Wilbraham: *The Englishman's Food, A History
of Five Centuries of English Diet,* p. 205.

decades comprising the first period of industrial capitalism, brought about a rapid deterioration of the conditions of the working class while at the same time the wealth of Britain, her productive capacity, her economic resources, increased rapidly. The ruling classes, among which the industrial capitalists assumed a more and more prominent place, became richer and more powerful while the masses of the people became poorer and were more suppressed.

The combination of bad harvests and the enclosure of common land was depriving many of their property, while the agricultural population, especially the agricultural workers, suffered severely from the widening gap between rising prices and their earning capacity. Many villages began to die out. People could no longer hope to keep themselves alive in the countryside; they therefore began to move in ever-increasing numbers to the towns where the growth of manufacture and increased opportunity of employment appeared to promise them a chance to earn a living. The following table serves to illustrate the rapid development of the production of non-agricultural goods:*

PRODUCTION OF NON-AGRICULTURAL GOODS
(1913 = 100)

1720–29	2·1	1800–09	5·7
1760–69	2·6	1810–19	7·1
1770–79	3·0	1820–29	9·7
1780–89	3·5	1830–39	14·3
1790–99	4·6	1840–49	19·6

We observe that the rate of growth between the two decades 1760–69 and 1770–79 is almost the same as that between the preceding five decades, 1720–29 to 1760–69, taken together, and with almost every following decade the rate of growth increases. Industrial production was becoming the dominant feature of British economy; and to the many evils which capitalist agriculture had brought to the masses of the people those of industrial capitalism were now being added.

*   *   *

* Walther Hoffmann, "Ein Index der industriellen Production für Grossbritannien seit dem 18. Jahrhundert." *Weltwirtschaftliches Archiv*, 40. Band, 1934, II, pp. 396–97.

In order to study conditions among the working class since the beginning of the industrial revolution we have to observe as many features and determining factors of their life as possible. While wages, for instance, especially if compared with the development of prices, give us some indication of their earning power, they do not tell us anything about housing conditions, the extent of child labour or the length of the working day. In the following pages, therefore, we shall try to assemble data on the main aspects of the life of the working class and the changes affecting it from the industrial revolution up to the middle of the last century; that is, up to the end of the first period of industrial capitalism.

⁕   *   *

The following two tables indicate the development of wages during the period under review.

WAGES IN INDIVIDUAL INDUSTRIES, 1779 TO 1849*

(1850 = 100)

Decades and Trade Cycles	London Artisans	Cotton Industry	Building Trades	Engineering Shipbuilding	Agriculture
1779–88	70	—	58	—	—
1789–98	75	—	66	—	83
1799–1808	88	182	—	—	111
1809–18	109	137	—	97†	120
1819–26	105	101	—	96	97
1820–26	105	100	—	96	95
1827–32	103	90	91	91	91
1833–42	99	93	95	—	91
1843–49	98	100	99	102	96

AVERAGE MONEY WAGES, COST OF LIVING, AND REAL WAGES*

(1850 = 100)

Decades and Trade Cycles	Money Wages	Cost of Living	Real Wages
1779–88	—	85	—
1789–98	94	97	98
1799–1808	114	137	83
1809–18	114	159	72
1819–26	99	125	79
1820–26	98	122	80
1827–32	93	114	82
1833–42	95	110	86
1843–49	98	109	90

* Wages by individual years, see Appendix to Chapter I, 1750 to 1850.
† 1810–18.

During the sixty years or more under review real wages first declined by about one quarter and then slowly rose again, but remained by almost 10 per cent below the real wage level at the beginning of the period. At about the middle of the nineteenth century, a worker could buy with his wages 10 per cent less than could his predecessor at the end of the eighteenth century; and had we the necessary data for the period between 1750 and 1789, we would probably find that the decline in the standard of purchasing power was even greater than the above figures indicate.

The decline up to 1818 was largely due, of course, to the economic crisis brought about by the wars against the French Revolution and Napoleon. Rapid rises in prices caused rapid falls in real wages. Yet—the more than thirty years following this period of wars and crises did not suffice to make up for the loss in real wages. In spite of rapidly increasing wealth, in spite of rapid technological progress and rapidly expanding industrial production, conditions among the working class remained worse than at the beginning of the industrial revolution.

If we look at the wages paid in individual industries we find that the general tendency is the same in all branches except the cotton industry. In the seventies and eighties wages are fairly stable and so is the cost of living. Beginning with the nineties up to the end of the wars with France, wages rise higher and higher while the cost of living mounts even more quickly. From then on to the middle of the thirties wages decline and the cost of living goes down even more than wages; the following years show a slight increase in wages. The different development in the cotton industry which paid lower and lower wages up to the thirties was due to technological changes in the industry, the rapid technical progress, the change-over from home to factory work, from manual to machine work, the pressure upon the wages of male workers by the especially rapid influx of women and children (though at the same time wages of male workers were depressed in order to force them to send wife and children into the factories); all this enabled the textile industry to pay particularly low wages instead of more or less the same as in other industries.

Almost all the above wage data refer to a full-time working

week. But during the period under review there were many years when unemployment rose steeply while there were others when the labour supply was almost insufficient. These changes in the situation are not reflected in the above figures, which should be corrected accordingly. Unfortunately, however, no accurate data are available as to variations in unemployment, and one of the few statements one can make with a certain assurance is that if we took unemployment into account the increase of real wages between 1833–42 and 1843–49 would be decidedly smaller, if not even wiped out.

Unemployment, especially its rapid rise during periods of industrial crisis, not only means loss of wages. It also means a terrible insecurity of livelihood.

Carlyle wrote as follows on the uncertainty in which the cotton spinner lives:*

"Their trade, now in plethoric prosperity, anon extenuated into inanition and 'short time,' is of the nature of gambling; they live by it like gamblers, now in luxurious superfluity, now in starvation. Black mutinous discontent devours them; simply the miserablest feeling that can inhabit the heart of man."

And Engels wrote:†

"But far more demoralizing than his poverty in its influence upon the English working-man is the insecurity of his position, the necessity of living upon wages from hand to mouth, that in short which makes a proletarian of him."

The attitude of the employers towards the misery of the unemployed workers is described in *The Times*, December 14, 1841:

"The mill-owners, or, as they have been not inaptly designated, the millocrats, of the midland counties assembled on Thursday last at Derby, in what is called by them a 'Great Conference,' for the purpose of clubbing their information respecting the influence of the corn laws upon their manufactures; and after a morning consumed in detailing the sufferings of unemployed artisans these gentlemen proceeded to celebrate the public

---

* *Chartism*, 2nd ed., p. 34.
† Friedrich Engels, *The Condition of the Working-Class in England in 1844*, London, 1936, p. 116.

distress which had brought them together in 'an excellent dinner, provided by the landlord of the Royal Hotel.' "

*   *   *

Besides unemployment there are further factors which reduce wages below the level indicated by the above figures, occasionally or over the period as a whole. One of them is the development of the system of fines. In order to "improve discipline," in order to take as much as possible from the workers, the employers began in the course of the period under review to work out a system of fines which made it possible to reduce actual wages paid to the workers to an increasing degree. Among the reasons for fines were: a worker found dirty at work, and a worker found washing himself in the factory; the amount of the fine for these two crimes was sometimes one shilling or even more, or about half of his daily earnings. If a worker in a spinning factory fell ill and could not find a satisfactory substitute for the day he often had to pay for the steam "unnecessarily produced," which might be as much as half his weekly wage.

Another device used by the employers in order to get back as much as possible from the wages they had to pay was the use of the truck system. This compels the worker to buy in company-controlled stores at prices far above normal. Often the workers received up to two-thirds of their wages in goods (foodstuffs, soap, candles, etc.) and when they rebelled against this practice they were severely punished. It is true, a number of Acts were in existence, forbidding the truck system; but the magistrates were not able to enforce them since the employers declined to obey the law, and the magistrates were either the employers themselves, or their relatives and friends. When the workers struck for the enforcement of the law or tried other means to compel the employers to obey the law of the country, they were imprisoned, flogged, or transported to penal settlements overseas on grounds of violation of the Vagrancy Acts.

Even if the workers got their full wages and could buy the goods they wanted in the open market, and even if they were able to avoid the imposition of fines, they were cheated in yet another fashion: the quality of the food they bought declined considerably in the period under review:

"There is indisputable evidence that a marked deterioration occurred in the eighteenth century in the quality of many foodstuffs, particularly those likely to be bought by the poorer people. It can to some extent be ascribed to the rapid commercialization of the trade in food which developed with the growth of the towns, and for this reason it was noticeable even in the first half of the century when the country as a whole was prosperous. It became much more striking, and its effects much more serious, when the dearth and high prices of the second fifty years brought greater temptation to the unscrupulous."*
"At no period have contemporary records shown the merchants to be guilty of such flagrant adulteration as between 1800 and 1850."†

Conditions deteriorated considerably in the second half of the eighteenth century and seem to have reached their lowest point in the first half of the nineteenth century. Loaves were doctored with alum, which increased the size and "improved" the colour (making them appear whiter); milk was of such incredibly poor quality, poisoned by adulterants or infection, that physicians recommended tea instead of this dangerous fluid; butter contained up to 33 per cent water and was often rancid.

But not only did the quality of the foodstuffs deteriorate. The decline in real wages also meant—as compared with conditions in the eighteenth century—a deterioration in the composition of the diet. Animal food formed an increasingly smaller proportion of the diet and Engels thus described food conditions among industrial workers:

"Descending gradually, we find the animal food reduced to a small piece of bacon cut up with the potatoes; lower still, even this disappears, and there remain only bread, cheese, porridge, and potatoes, until on the lowest round of the ladder, among the Irish, potatoes form the sole food."‡ "The food is, in general, bad; often almost unfit for use, and in many cases, at least at times, insufficient in quantity, so that, in extreme cases, death by starvation results."§

In other communities, bread takes the place of potatoes as the chief nourishment. "The staple food of the working man was

* J. C. Drummond and Anne Wilbraham, l.c. pp. 221–22.
† L.c. p. 341.   ‡ Friedrich Engels, l.c. p. 72.   § L.c. p. 74.

still bread. Often in the hard times, particularly early in the nineteenth century, it was all he got. . . ."[*]

A further development which limited the purchasing power of the worker and which finds no expression in the above wage tables is the following: During the greater part of the eighteenth century, a great many workers had a small garden plot where they could raise some vegetables or even rear a pig. With increasing industrialization and urbanization, with the swarming of large numbers of the industrial working class into congested cities, where houses were close together and space too valuable to be left open, this additional source of income ceased, and the workers remained wholly dependent upon their wage earnings. True, the percentage of industrial workers who got some additional food from such garden plots or pieces of land was still considerable around the middle of the nineteenth century, but it was undoubtedly much lower than around 1790.

*   *   *

Though wages, even real wages, are, as we have said above, an important factor in the life of the worker, they are not the decisive factor. Did other factors move in a way which mitigated or even compensated and over-compensated for the unfavourable development of wages? "A poor man, under one system of life, may be happier than a man who is less poor under another, for civilization is the complex of all the forces and conditions that inspire and govern imagination and conduct."[†]

One may say: Wages and real wages declined yet family earnings probably increased. A worker's family of man, wife and three children, aged five, seven and twelve years, probably earned in 1830 as much as in 1790. But in 1790 very probably only the man worked, and at most his wife and the twelve-year-old child would contribute to the family earnings. In 1830, however, we may be sure that the seven-year-old child, and possibly also the five-year-old, had to work as well. The low wages of the men (especially their decline in the textile industries)

* J. C. Drummond and Anne Wilbraham, l.c. p. 388.
† J. L. Hammond and Barbara Hammond, *The Town Labourer*, *1760–1832*, London, 1937, pp. 6–7.

and the working opportunities which the new factory system created, forced the families to take their small children into the factories.

In the period of industrial capitalism under review the employment of women and children increased very rapidly. A manifesto from the Female Political Union of Newcastle,* in 1839, explained that men's wages were so low that the mother and her small children were driven to work at a labour that degraded soul and body, and if this were not compulsion enough the overseers gave jobs only to men bringing a child with them. One can even say that for some time child labour formed the basis of the factory system. Certain kinds of work, especially in the textile industries, was done only by children; and according to opinion among the ruling classes this was perfectly right. William Pitt, Prime Minister around the turn of the century, proposed in his Poor Law Bill that children should start work at the age of five; and since the work required only a low mental equipment, a Lancashire millowner readily agreed to take one idiot with every twenty children furnished him by a London parish. In the factories and mines the children worked for twelve or even more hours. Often they slept in the factories or fell asleep beside the machines during their working hours; innumerable accidents happened in this way.

If the children were too young to work in the mills or factories, and if no member of the family was unemployed, the children were left at home alone and were often drugged in order to keep them "safe and quiet." The drugs bore significant names, such as Infant's Preservative and Mother's Blessing.

Often, especially during periods of crisis and depression, the man had to stay at home—unemployed—while the wife and the children had to go to work at shamelessly low wages:†

"In many cases the family is not wholly dissolved by the employment of the wife, but turned upside down. The wife supports the family, the husband sits at home, tends the children, sweeps the room and cooks. This case happens very frequently; in Manchester alone, many hundred such men could be cited, condemned to domestic occupations. It is easy to imagine the wrath aroused among the working-men by this reversal of all

* *Northern Star*, February 9, 1839   † Engels, l.c. p. 144.

relations within the family, while the other social conditions remain unchanged."

While an increasing proportion of the family was condemned to factory work, the number of hours worked also increased. Working days of 14, 16 and even 18 hours could be noted in many a factory during the thirties and even in the forties, while in the eighties of the eighteenth century such a working day was exceptional and evocative of comment. In Lancashire, for instance, a twelve-hour day was an exceptionally short working day in the twenties, while forty years before it was regarded as exceptionally long. Karl Marx pungently writes :*

". . . With this end in view, and for the purpose of 'extirpating idleness, debauchery, and excess,' of promoting a spirit of industry, of 'lowering the price of labour in our manufactories, and easing the lands of the heavy burden of poor's rates,' our faithful champion of capital advocates a well-tried means. The workers who become dependent on public support, paupers in a word, are to be confined in 'an ideal workhouse.' Such an ideal workhouse must be made 'a House of Terror,' and not an asylum for the poor, not a place 'where they are to be plentifully fed, warmly and decently clothed, and where they do but little work.' In this 'House of Terror,' this 'ideal workhouse,' the poor 'shall work fourteen hours in a day, allowing proper time for meals, in such manner that there shall remain twelve hours of neat labour.' . . . Twelve working hours daily in an 'ideal workhouse,' in a 'House of Terror.' Such was a proposal made in 1770! Sixty-three years later, in 1833, when in four branches of industry the working day for children at ages ranging from thirteen to eighteen was by legal enactment reduced to twelve full working hours, a clamour was raised as if the knell of doom had sounded for English industry."

The lengthening of the working day, which brought rapidly increasing profits to the ruling classes, was morally justified by reiterating that if the workers had more leisure they would not know how to spend it profitably and would degenerate morally. "All experience proves that in the lower orders the deterioration of morals increases with the quantity of unemployed time of

* *Capital*, Dent's edition, pp. 281, 282.

which they have the command."* And what holds true of the adults is even truer of the children. Mr. G. A. Lee, a cotton mill owner, put it neatly: "Nothing is more favourable to morals than habits of early subordination, industry, and regularity."†

Another factor which contributed to a serious deterioration of the standard of living of the working class during the period under review was the rapid congestion in towns and cities. The industrialization of the country led to a rapid flow from the agricultural districts, and the "deserted village" had its counterpart in the over-crowded city. Engels describes housing conditions in a part of London in the beginning of the forties:

"It is a disorderly collection of tall, three- or four-storied houses with narrow, crooked, filthy streets. . . . The houses are occupied from cellar to garret, filthy within and without, and their appearance is such that no human being could possibly wish to live in them. But all this is nothing in comparison with the dwellings in the narrow courts and alleys between the streets, entered by covered passages between the houses, in which the filth and tottering ruin surpass all description. Scarcely a whole window-pane can be found, the walls are crumbling, door-posts and window-frames loose and broken. . . . Heaps of garbage and ashes lie in all directions, and the foul liquids emptied before the doors gather in stinking pools."‡

And summarizing a housing survey of Manchester, Engels says:§

"In a word, we must confess that in the working-men's dwellings of Manchester, no cleanliness, no convenience, and consequently no comfortable family life is possible; that in such dwellings only a physically degenerate race, robbed of all humanity, degraded, reduced morally and physically to bestiality, could feel comfortable and at home."

In the country housing conditions were no less terrible. Cobbett described them:

"The labourers seem miserably poor. Their dwellings are little better than pig-beds, and their looks indicate that their

* "An Inquiry into the Principle and Tendency of the Bill for imposing certain restrictions on Cotton Factories, 1818."

† Quoted by J. L. and Barbara Hammond, l.c. pp. 180, 181.

‡ Friedrich Engels, l.c. p. 27.   § L.c. p. 63.

food is not nearly equal to that of a pig. Their wretched hovels
are stuck upon little bits of ground on the road side, where the
space has been wider than the road demanded. In many places
they have not two rods to a hovel. . . . In my whole life I never
saw human wretchedness equal to this: no, not even amongst
the free negroes in America, who, on the average, do not work
one day out of four. And, this is 'prosperity,' is it? These, oh
Pitt! are the fruits of thy hellish system!"*

As a result of the increase in the working hours, the intensified
physical exhaustion of the worker and growing undernourish-
ment, the number of accidents in the factories and mines
increased. True, some technical progress was made which
might have contributed to a decline in industrial accidents.
But such progress was employed as an instrument even further
to increase profits for the ruling classes and to exhaust the
labour power of the workers:

". . . Hodgson's action led to the establishment of a Society
at Sunderland for preventing accidents, and it was in answer to
an appeal from this Society that Sir Humphry Davy. visited
Newcastle and gave his mind to the problem. Unfortunately
even the alleviations of science were turned to the miner's
disadvantage. The Davy lamp, for which the inventor refused
to take out a patent, renouncing an income of £5,000 or £10,000
a year, 'his sole object to serve the cause of humanity,' was used
in many cases to serve the cause of profits. Deeper and more
dangerous seams were worked, and accidents actually increased
in number. The writer of *A Voice from the Coal Mines*, a pamphlet
published by the Northumberland miners in 1825, stated that
since the introduction of the lamp the miner had had to work
in still higher temperatures under conditions that caused him
physical agony."†

*   *   *

Life for the workers in the factories and mines and in the
field, grew worse and worse. This development alone meant a
considerable deterioration of the mental life and morale of the

---

* William Cobbett, *Rural Rides*, November 7, 1821. 1885 edition, p. 21.
† J. L. and Barbara Hammond, l.c. pp. 37, 38.

workers. In addition, however, the ruling classes did everything
possible to reduce the cultural standards of the masses. Not only
did they strenuously oppose all educational progress; they also
sought to reduce the standard of education by the progressive
reduction of the workers' leisure periods and by reducing the
standards of such educational institutions as did exist. Mr.
Giddy, M.P., President of the Royal Society, argued as follows:

"However specious in theory the project might be, of giving
education to the labouring classes of the poor, it would in
effect be found to be prejudicial to their morals and happiness;
it would teach them to despise their lot in life, instead of making
them good servants in agriculture, and other labourious employ-
ments to which their rank in society had destined them; instead
of teaching them subordination, it would render them factious
and refractory, as was evident in the manufacturing counties;
it would enable them to read seditious pamphlets, vicious books,
and publications against Christianity; it would render them
insolent to their superiors; and in a few years the result would
be that the legislature would find it necessary to direct the
strong arm of power towards them, and to furnish the executive
magistrate with much more vigorous laws than were now in
force."*

But should any member of the labouring class by some
fortuitous event or by diligent self-schooling become able to read,
then the right kind of literature must be on hand for him. Not
seditious pamphlets which might induce him to reflect upon his
lot, to compare his condition with that of the rich, to discuss
changes in his condition, but tempered discursions to show that
he was really much better off than his employer, and that the
poor had every reason to be much happier than the rich.

"Some of the necessities which poverty (if the condition of
the labouring part of mankind must be so called) imposes, are
not hardships but pleasure. Frugality itself is a pleasure. It is
an exercise of attention and contrivance, which, whenever it is
successful, produces satisfaction. The very care and forecast that
are necessary to keep expenses and earnings upon a level form,
when not embarrassed by too great difficulties, an agreeable

* Hansard, IX, p. 798 nn.; quoted by J. L. and Barbara Hammond, l.c.
p. 70.

engagement of the thoughts. This is lost amidst abundance. There is no pleasure in taking out of a large unmeasured fund. They who do that, and only that, are the mere conveyers of money from one hand to another. A yet more serious advantage which persons in inferior stations possess, is the ease with which they provide for their children. All the provision which a poor man's child requires is contained in two words, 'industry and innocence.' With these qualities, though without a shilling to set him forwards, he goes into the world prepared to become a useful, virtuous, and happy man. Nor will he fail to meet with a maintenance adequate to the habits with which he has been brought up, and to the expectations which he has formed; a degree of success sufficient for a person of any condition whatever."

Thus wrote Archdeacon William Paley in his *Reasons for Contentment; Addressed to the Labouring Part of the British Public.** It must be added that his pamphlet had many readers, that the author was considered eminently sane and that he died a natural death; he was, in fact, a famous theologian well beloved by the ruling classes.

But not all shared the opinions of Giddy and Paley. There were employers who regarded education as desirable—but unfortunately, they argued, it could not be achieved because to take an hour or two from the working time of the children would spell financial disaster, would mean "the surrender of all the profits of the establishment."

In concluding this survey of conditions of the working class between 1750 and 1850 we find it correct to say that "the poorer people knew hard times in the second half of the eighteenth century,"† and that it is equally correct that. "One does not have to look far to find evidence that during the first twenty-five years of the nineteenth century the condition of the poorer people, both in town and country, went from bad to worse."‡

This deterioration was due not only to the fact that the wages of the workers declined in purchasing power, but also to other harmful changes in working and living conditions. Accidents

---

* 1792 edition, pp. 11, 12. The pamphlet ran through several editions up to 1819.

† J. C. Drummond and Anne Wilbraham, l.c. p. 261.   ‡ L.c. p. 331.

increased, the working day was continually being lengthened, wherever labour power existed—be it among women or children, the sound or the sick, the sane or the feeble-minded—full use was made of it. It was a period of extensive exploitation, brutal, ruthless, primitive. If workers became incapacitated, if children fell sick or were disabled, if women broke down, it did not much matter—one could get others. If, because of the length of the working day, general fatigue lowered output, it did not much matter: one simply lengthened the working day again without increasing wages.*

But the fact that exploitation increased extensively, that is that the creation of absolute surplus value played an increasing role, must not blind us to the fact that, at the same time, relative surplus value was produced—that is, that the working process became more and more intensive.† By various means the process of production was speeded up, and often the intensity of work per hour was also increased. One of the most tragic examples of this intensification of the working process was the beating of children in the factories by their parents in order to keep them awake or drive them to work faster. But these parents beat their children only to save them from a more cruel beating by the overseers, who used for this purpose the "billy-roller," a heavy iron stick.

In fact, if workers stayed away from work, even if only to sleep off a drinking bout, it contributed to a slight improvement

* "The inherent tendency of capitalist production, therefore, is towards the appropriation of labour for the whole twenty-four hours of the day." (Karl Marx, l.c. p. 259).

† Surplus value is the value which the workers produce above the value of their wages. Assuming their wages being roughly sufficient to keep them alive and able to work, and assuming that the workers work about 6 hours in order to produce sufficient goods to keep them alive and able to work, all other things which they produce during the rest of the working day go to their employers and are surplus value, value above what is needed to keep them alive and able to work, value above the value of their wages. Surplus value can be created and increased by increasing the length of the working day. Surplus value created and increased in such a way is called absolute surplus value. Or, the employers may succeed in shortening the number of hours necessary to produce the minimum of goods needed to keep the workers alive and able to work (e.g. from six to five hours). They may do this either through technical progress and/or by increasing the intensity of work. If the total length of the working day remains the same, the surplus value created by the workers may, then, increase considerably. Surplus value created in such a way is called relative surplus value.

in their health conditions. Engels* quotes Dr. Knight of Sheffield about conditions among grinders:

"I can convey some idea of the injuriousness of this occupation only by asserting that the hardest drinkers among the grinders are the longest lived among them, because they are longest and oftenest absent from their work."

"The depreciation of human life was thus the leading fact about the new system for the working classes. The human material was used up rapidly; workmen were called old at forty; the arrangements of society ensured an infinite supply; women and children were drawn in, arid at the end the working class, which was now contributing not only the men but the entire family, seemed to be what it was at the beginning, a mere part of the machinery without share in the increased wealth or the increased power over life that machinery had brought. For the revolution that had raised the standard of comfort for the rich had depressed the standard of life for the poor; it had given to the capitalist a new importance, while it had degraded the workpeople to be the mere muscles of industry."†

*   *   *

During the period under review the industrial working class was still young and without much experience. The French Revolution was a revolution of the class already in power in Britain, of the bourgeoisie. Reliable information on events in France was scarce, and the masses could not read. Yet unrest among the masses was so great that new Combination Laws had to be passed designed to safeguard the employers against organized working-class action. Pitt spoke of remedies for an "evil of considerable magnitude." Through these Combination Laws, which in effect made every strike or other form of organized resistance against wage cuts or increased working hours, against the imposition of new fines or harsh treatment by the overseers, legally impossible, and which led to the severe punishment of many a courageous fighter for the interests of his class, the employers were able to repress the labour movement and impede its development. Consequently, they had almost

* Engels, l.c. p. 203.   † J. L. and Barbara Hammond, l.c. p. 50.

unlimited freedom to impose the harshest working and living conditions upon the workers.

George White and Gravener Henson, in their anonymously published *A Few Remarks on the State of the Laws at present in Existence for Regulating Masters and Workpeople* (1823), describe the Act of 1800, in the new textile industries, as being "a tremendous millstone round the neck of the local artisan, which has depressed and debased him to the earth: every act which he has attempted, every measure that he has devised to keep up or raise his wages, he has been told was illegal: the whole force of the civil power and influence of the district has been exerted against him because he was acting illegally: the magistrates, acting, as they believed, in unison with the views of the legislature, to check and keep down wages and combination, regarded, in almost every instance, every attempt on the part of the artisan to ameliorate his situation or support his station in society as a species of sedition and resistance of the Government: every committee or active man among them was regarded as a turbulent, dangerous instigator, whom it was necessary to watch and crush if possible."

A good example of the effects of the Combination Laws was the strike of the Scottish cotton weavers in 1812 for fixed wage rates, perhaps the largest strike in this period. Forty thousand weavers were on strike for three weeks. Towards the end, the employers appeared to be yielding, when suddenly the whole strike committee was arrested and the five leaders received prison sentences for the crime of combination. This broke the strike.

There were numerous strikes in this period. Occasionally thousands of workers would take part in one. Sometimes the strike was carefully prepared by one of the numerous short-lived unions formed at this time. But most of these strikes were unsuccessful and no coherent labour movement grew out of them. This holds true particularly of the factory workers. Sidney and Beatrice Webb, who perhaps regard conditions among the handicraftsmen too favourably, write:

"In place of the steady organized resistance to encroachment maintained by the handicraftsmen, we watch, in the machine industries, the alternation of outbursts of machine-breaking and outrages, with intervals of abject submission and reckless competition with each other for employment. In the conduct of such organization as there was, repressive laws had, with the operatives as with the London artisans, the effect of throwing great power into the hands of a few men. These leaders were implicitly obeyed in times of industrial conflict, but the repeated defeats which they were unable to avert prevented that growth of confidence which is indispensable for permanent organization."*

Engels writes:†

"The history of these Unions is a long series of defeats of the working-men, interrupted by a few isolated victories."

However, though unorganized and usually unsuccessful, the general pressure of the masses was so strong that in 1825 Parliament decided to repeal the Combination Laws. Though trade unions were not made legal by the new Act, the right to collective bargaining and the right to strike were established. The movement for the repeal of the Combination Laws and for other progressive acts in the twenties, thirties and forties of the nineteenth century was to a great extent headed by a number of bourgeois Radicals, liberal humanitarians, men of progressive ideas. The ruling class permitted them to operate because a change in industrial conditions, in the technique of exploitation, was in progress, and these reformers did partly the work of advertising as moral progress the measures, the introduction of which technical progress and new methods of exploitation required anyway. This general explanation of why these Radicals were successful does not detract in any degree from their courage, their usefulness and resolution. They were great men; and in the preface to *Capital*, Karl Marx pays well-merited tribute to those who worked as factory inspectors, medical investigators into the public health, commissioners of inquiry into the exploitation of women and children, housing conditions, the food supply, and so on.

During the last ten or twelve years of the period we are reviewing, the organized Trade Union movement and the general Radical movement led by bourgeois progressives—which two

* *The History of Trade Unionism* (Revised edition, extended to 1920), p. 87.
† L.c. p. 216.

had frequently been interrelated—now merged into the great Chartist movement.

The Chartist movement transformed strikes into political rebellions. It gave substantial backing to political movements by the calling of strikes in their support. It conceived the idea of organizing a general strike in order to transform the political machinery of the country, and sought to bring about a political revolution to secure power for the people. The breaking-up of the Chartist movement also signifies the termination of the first period of the industrial labour movement, a period marked by almost continuous defeat on the industrial field, but by certain successes in Parliament çaused, not by any sudden burgeoning of humanitarianism among the ruling class, but by their fear of the masses and by changes in the methods of industrial production.

APPENDIX TO CHAPTER I
1750 TO 1850

I. TABLES

1. WAGES IN AGRICULTURE AND INDUSTRY AND THE COST OF LIVING FROM 1775 TO 1850

(1850 = 100)

Year	London Artisans	Cotton Industry	Building Trades	Engineering Shipbuilding	Agriculture	All Workers	Cost of Living
1775	70	—	55	—	—	—	84
1776	70	—	56	—	—	—	78
1777	70	—	56	—	—	—	85
1778	70	—	55	—	—	—	82
1779	70	—	56	—	—	—	78
1780	70	—	56	—	—	—	73
1781	70	—	56	—	—	—	87
1782	70	—	58	—	—	—	91
1783	70	—	58	—	—	—	90
1784	70	—	56	—	—	—	88
1785	70	—	58	—	—	—	86
1786	70	—	60	—	—	—	84
1787	70	—	58	—	—	—	84
1788	70	—	60	—	—	—	84
1789	70	—	60	—	71	84	86

1. WAGES IN AGRICULTURE AND INDUSTRY AND THE COST OF LIVING FROM 1775 TO 1850—*continued*

(1850 = 100)

Year	London Artisans	Cotton Industry	Building Trades	Engineering Shipbuilding	Agriculture	All Workers	Cost of Living
1790	72	—	60	—	73	86	91
1791	72	—	60	—	75	87	88
1792	72	—	63	—	77	89	87
1793	73	—	69	54	79	93	92
1794	75	—	69	—	83	96	94
1795	78	—	69	—	87	99	108
1796	79	—	69	—	90	101	108
1797	81	177	69	—	94	104	107
1798	82	187	69	—	96	105	108
1799	82	175	69	—	98	106	116
1800	82	177	—	76	100	107	145
1801	84	175	—	—	102	108	148
1802	85	199	—	76	104	115	125
1803	85	189	—	—	108	113	130
1804	86	189	—	—	113	115	131
1805	88	217	—	87	119	125	144
1806	88	189	—	—	121	118	140
1807	97	168	—	—	123	118	140
1808	101	139	—	—	123	112	147
1809	103	145	—	—	123	115	161
1810	106	148	—	98	123	118	162
1811	111	132	—	94	123	114	160
1812	111	146	—	94	123	117	175
1813	112	153	—	98	123	120	180
1814	113	179	—	98	121	126	163
1815	113	142	—	98	119	117	147
1816	108	117	—	98	117	109	143
1817	106	106	—	98	115	105	147
1818	106	102	—	97	112	103	148
1819	104	102	—	99	112	103	146
1820	103	102	—	96	108	101	137
1821	104	101	—	96	102	100	126
1822	104	101	—	96	94	98	113
1823	104	100	—	96	90	96	115
1824	106	101	—	96	90	97	117
1825	107	101	—	96	90	97	127
1826	106	97	—	96	92	97	122
1827	106	97	92	94	92	96	120
1828	105	94	92	92	92	95	116
1829	103	94	91	91	90	94	114

1. WAGES IN AGRICULTURE AND INDUSTRY AND THE COST OF LIVING FROM 1775 TO 1850—continued

(1850 = 100)

Year	London Artisans	Cotton Industry*	Building Trades	Engineering Shipbuilding	Agriculture	All Workers	Cost of Living
1830	104	87	91	89	90	92	108
1831	101	85	91	89	90	91	114
1832	101	86	91	90	92	92	112
1833	101	88	91	91	92	93	107
1834	101	94	91	91	90	94	103
1835	100	90	91	—	87	92	101
1836	98	92	93	—	88	93	106
1837	98	94	95	—	88	94	113
1838	98	94	97	—	90	96	113
1839	98	94	98	—	90	96	121
1840	98	94	98	102	92	97	115
1841	98	97	98	102	94	98	119
1842	98	97	98	100	96	98	104
1843	99	97	98	100	96	98	103
1844	99	99	98	102	94	99	103
1845	98	105	98	102	94	99	107
1846	98	105	98	103	96	100	117
1847	98	98	98	103	98	99	122
1848	98	98	100	101	98	99	110
1849	99	99	100	100	98	93	104
1850	100	100	100	100	100	100	100

2. REAL WAGES 1789–1850

(1850 = 100)

Year	Real Wages	Year	Real Wages	Year	Real Wages	Year	Real Wages
1789	98	1805	86	1820	74	1835	91
		1806	84	1821	79	1836	88
1790	95	1807	84	1822	86	1837	84
1791	99	1808	76	1823	84	1838	85
1792	103	1809	71	1824	83	1839	79
1793	101						
1794	102	1810	73	1825	77	1840	84
		1811	71	1826	79	1841	82
1795	91	1812	67	1827	80	1842	94
1796	94	1813	67	1828	82	1843	95
1797	97	1814	78	1829	82	1844	96
1798	97						
1799	91	1815	79	1830	86	1845	93
		1816	76	1831	80	1846	85
1800	74	1817	72	1832	82	1847	81
1801	73	1818	69	1833	87	1848	90
1802	91	1819	71	1834	91	1849	89
1803	87						
1804	88					1850	100

II. Sources and Remarks.

An immense amount of useful information and the most penetrating appreciation of labour conditions in the period reviewed in Chapter I are to be found in Karl Marx's *Capital* and in Friedrich Engels' *The Condition of the Working-Class in England in 1844*; most useful also, are: Sidney and Beatrice Webb, *The History of Trade Unionism*; J. L. and Barbara Hammond, *The Town Labourer, 1760–1832*; and J. C. Drummond and Anne Wilbraham, *The Englishman's Food, Five Centuries of English Diet*.

The wage statistics are based on the studies of A. L. Bowley and G. H. Wood, entitled "The Statistics of Wages in the United Kingdom during the last Hundred Years," and published in the *Journal of the Royal Statistical Society*, 1899 to 1910; on Mr. Bowley's book *Wages in the United Kingdom in the Nineteenth Century*; on the official wage collection *Returns of Wages, Published between 1830 and 1886*, London, 1887; on Mrs. E. W. Gilboy's study, *Wages in Eighteenth-Century England*; and on the all too short article by R. S. Tucker, "Real Wages of Artisans in London, 1729–1935," in the *Journal of the American Statistical Association*, Vol. 31, No. 193, March 1936. The latter also contains the cost of living index which we have used.

Wage statistics relating to the period are of relatively low quality. The index of wages for all workers is based on a small number of industries only, and important industries, as for instance coal mining, are missing. Industries included in the survey are often represented only by skilled workers in a few occupations. No data on time lost through unemployment, short time, strikes and accidents are available. Some of the figures refer to wage rates, others to full-time earnings. Changes-over from male labour to female and child labour have not been taken into account. Wage data are overweighted with material from the big cities, especially London, and from the bigger establishments. The cost of living index refers exclusively to London.

The different series of indices have not been weighted, with the exception of the years 1800 to 1810 when, because of missing data, "Engineering and Shipbuilding" dropped out while the

cotton industry with its unusual movement of wages remained;
I weighted "London Artisans" by 2, the other indices keeping
their weight of 1.

The index of wages for all workers is a chain-index; the chain
was constructed backwards, beginning with 1850; this explains
why the index of wages of all workers in 1789, for example, is
84, while the three indices from which the general index is
composed are 71 or less.

It is obvious from these observations that the statistical
picture given is a very rough one. On the other hand, it would
be hasty and incorrect to conclude that the *trend* indicated by
the above tables is wrong. Wage conditions and real wage
conditions did develop in the directions indicated in the above
tables.

As compared with those given in my book *Labour Conditions in
Western Europe* the above figures are better, as I have been able
to make use of the study by Mr. Tucker and of many valuable
suggestions received since the publication of my former study.
If we compare the development of real wages according to both
my former and the present studies, we arrive at the following
table:

REAL WAGES, 1820 TO 1850

(1820–26 = 100)

Trade Cycle	Former Study	Corrected Data
1820–26	100	100
1827–32	98	102
1833–42	114	108
1843–49	121	113

The improvement in the corrected data is due chiefly to a
decided improvement in the cost-of-living index through the
use of that constructed by Mr. Tucker. The two cost-of-living
indices run as follows:

COST OF LIVING, 1820 TO 1850

(1820–26 = 100)

Trade Cycle	Former Study	Corrected Data
1820–26	100	100
1827–32	98	93
1833–42	87	90
1843–49	85	89

The larger decline in the cost of living between 1820–26 and 1827–32 in the corrected index leads to a small increase of real wages instead of the small decline which my former study indicated; the smaller decline in the cost of living during the following trade cycle period leads to a smaller increase in real wages than in my former study.

Just as soon as we were able to discern regular trade cycles, I have given trade cycle averages instead of ten-year-averages. In this way I have avoided having one average (as could be the case with a ten-year one) contain, for example, two instances of wages pulled down by the heavy falls of two crises while the next average does not contain a single year of deep crisis. This innovation, which I introduced in my former books, has found general approval.

CHAPTER II

1850 TO 1900

THE beginnings of the new period in the development of industrial capitalism and of labour conditions can already be discerned during the first half of the nineteenth century.

Its chief characteristics were the changing methods of production and exploitation in Britain, chief emphasis being given to the intensification of the working process (with more widespread use of machinery and the use of more and more complex machinery) and the production of relative surplus value: a shorter working day but more work per hour; employment of a smaller percentage of the working population (fewer children and in some industries fewer women) but better training for those employed (with better and more widespread elementary education); increasing real wages and increasing exploitation. Related to this are the creation of a labour aristocracy and a solid trade union movement among the skilled workers; and large-scale exportation of capital into the colonial empire, and as a consequence the increasing exploitation of natives by industrial capitalist methods (chiefly in mining, railway construction and on plantations).

The first indications of a change in the emphasis of methods of exploitation can be found in the early history of factory legislation. The first law referring to working conditions in factories was passed in 1802; it restricted the number of hours worked by apprentices in the cotton industry to twelve per day; up to 1833, three more Acts were passed: one in 1819, introducing the minimum age of nine for children in the cotton industry and limiting the working day for children between nine and and sixteen years of age to twelve hours per day; one in 1825, limiting the hours worked per week to sixty-nine and on Saturday to nine for children in the cotton industry; and one in 1831, prohibiting night work for young persons aged from nine to twenty-one and applying the 1825 Act to all persons under eighteen. But since Parliament did not vote any funds for adequate inspection of factories, since, also, parents had to abet the employers in violating these Acts because otherwise the family would have starved to death, and since there was no well organized labour movement to oppose infractions of these Acts, "The fact is that, prior to the Act of 1833, young persons and children were worked all night, all day, or both *ad libitum*."*

The next Act, that of 1833, referred to all textile branches, to children and to young persons, and limited the working day for children to forty-eight hours per week. Provision was made for inspection of factories, but the employers devised a system of employing the children in relays and starting the relays at irregular times, rendering it impossible for the inspectors to control the execution of the Act. Thus eleven more years passed without any effective factory legislation.

The first effective Act, passed in 1844, applied to textiles as a whole, and not only to children and young persons but also to adult women; it introduced the so-called half-time system for children, who were to work only six and a half hours daily or ten hours for three alternate days; women to work the same hours as young persons, that is, twelve hours daily and sixty-nine hours weekly.

These Acts, all dealing with the length of the working day, were designed to limit to a certain extent the rate of extensive exploitation, the production of absolute surplus value. But this limitation did not mean a limitation of profits. Quite early in the century, Robert Owen began to experiment with a shortened working day and to study its influence on output; he found that output per hour as well as output per day was not only maintained but even increased when he shortened the working day. He simply augmented the intensity of labour, and thus not only preserved but amplified the rate of exploitation by means of shortening the working day. Through the widening use of improved machinery, on the one hand, and, on the other, through the pressure of the working class for a shorter workday—pressure which was at first sporadic but which became, during the second half of the century, progressively stronger

* *Reports of Inspectors of Factories*, April 30, 1860, p. 50.

and better organized—the new form of exploitation, based chiefly on intensified labour and the increased production of relative instead of absolute surplus value, became universal.

Growing concern about the poor physique of the children, not for the children's sake, but for the sake of their future use as adult workers, helped to create an atmosphere not unfavourable to the effective introduction of factory legislation. Furthermore, the big employers began to realize that, while the new legislation forced them to improve technique by introducing better machinery, the same process would also help them, if the Factory Acts were applied throughout the whole industry, to eliminate the small employers who could not afford to buy new machinery. "Nevertheless, though the Factory Acts thus artificially ripen the material conditions requisite for the transformation of the manufacturing system into the factory system, at the same time, since they render a more considerable outlay of capital necessary, they hasten the decay of the small masters and the concentration of capital."*

Thus, it was not only to the advantage of the workers but also to that of the big employers as opposed to their smaller competitors, that, if factory legislation, once introduced, was to be observed, it should be observed in industry as a whole. This may have helped to make factory legislation relatively effective in the second half of the nineteenth century. The numerous Factory Acts passed during the period from the first effective piece of factory legislation in 1844 until the consolidation of factory legislation in 1901, all referred to children and/or young persons and/or women, and by 1867 the scope of their application embraced all workshops employing fifty or more workers. They dealt chiefly with the regulation of the working day, but also contained clauses on sanitary conditions, on prevention of accidents and the education of children.

There is no doubt that factory legislation improved working conditions in certain respects and for certain groups of workers. Though child labour did not definitely decline until late in the seventies,† working conditions for children improved. Though

* Karl Marx, *Capital*, p. 514.
† The percentage of children aged less than thirteen years working in textile industries was (cf. G. H. Wood, "Factory Legislation, considered with refer-

the shortening of the women's working day was, from the point of view of the employers, more than indemnified through intensification of the work performed, the additional leisure brought improvement into the lives of many women. True, the lessening in the number of hours worked by many adult male workers affected by factory legislation was richly amended, from the employers' point of view, by increased production of relative surplus value. But the new leisure afforded time for trade union activity. The consequent further benefits derived from trade union pressure for improvement in working conditions and all the advantages in home life which the gradual shortening of the working day brought about, contributed to the betterment of the life of the workers affected. One must, however, bear in mind the fact that the number of workers unaffected by factory legislation was very considerable.

*   *   *

The development of factory legislation has been put in the forefront of this discussion of labour conditions in the second half of the nineteenth century because it shows very clearly the new trend in the evolution of exploitation, namely: increased emphasis upon the creation of relative surplus value. This short survey should be supplemented by a study of the development of productivity per hour and per day in the industries affected by factory legislation, and in industry as a whole. Unfortunately, very few data are available on this subject, and they are not of the best quality. We shall therefore content ourselves with examples drawn from the cotton industry where such investigations are relatively easy because of the technical character of the industry and because of the interest which statisticians and economists have shown in this problem as affecting this industry. Fortunately, the cotton industry is also foremost in the history of factory legislation. The following table gives an index of the number of hours worked per week, and the production per operative in the cotton yarns and in the cotton goods depart-

ence to the Wages, etc., of the Operatives Protected thereby," *Journal of the Royal Statistical Society*, June 1902, p. 311): 1835, 13 per cent; 1839, 6 per cent; 1850, 6 per cent; 1856, 6 per cent; 1870, 9 per cent; 1874, 13 per cent; 1878, 11 per cent; 1885, 9 per cent; 1890, 8 per cent; 1895, 5 per cent.

ments, per year as well as per day; a second table gives the number of operatives per spindle and the number of looms worked by a weaver.*

THE DEVELOPMENT OF PRODUCTIVITY IN THE COTTON INDUSTRY

TABLE I

| | | Lbs. Production per Operative | | | |
| | | Cotton Yarns | | Cotton Goods | |
Years	Hours Worked per Week	per year	per hour	per year	per hour
1829–31	100	100	100	100	100
1844–46	87	178	205	323	372
1859–61	87	237	273	615	708
1880–82	82	357	436	775	948
1891–93	82	431	526	762	932

While the number of hours worked per week declined by almost 20 per cent, productivity per hour increased in some departments almost tenfold. The new policy of putting the chief emphasis on the production of relative surplus value, of decreasing the number of hours worked per worker and increasing in higher proportion the production per hour, is clearly revealed in the above table. Unfortunately, it is not possible to find out how much of the augmented production per hour is to be ascribed to increased intensity of labour and how much to technical progress, but that the intensity of work increased rapidly is beyond doubt. The following table supplements the data given above:

TABLE II

Number of Operatives per 1,000 spindles in a large concern		A Weaver Worked Looms	
Year	Number	Year	Number
1836	10	1820	0·9
1850	7·5	1850	1–2
1865	3·6	1878	2–3
1893	3·0	1885	3–4
		1893	4–6

The number of spindles served by a single operative thus increased by more than three times, while the number of looms

* Cf. F. Merttens, "On the Hours and Cost of Labour in the Cotton Industry at Home and Abroad," *Manchester Statistical Society*, 1893–94.

worked per operative rose by four and a half to seven times. Truly an astonishing development!

*   *   *

How did wages develop in this period of rapidly increasing production and productivity? The following table gives a survey of wages in individual industries:

WAGES IN INDIVIDUAL INDUSTRIES, 1849 TO 1903*

(1900 = 100)

Trade Cycle	Agricul- ture	Engineering Shipbuilding	Cotton	Textiles	Building	Printing	Coal Mining
1849–58	58	71	52	—	61	81	—
1859–68	68	75	66	—	70	81	—
1869–79	90	84	81	—	83	89	—
1880–86	86	86	84	92	87	94	64
1887–95	90	91	91	95	91	97	76
1895–1903	97	98	98	98	98	100	83

Wages moved rather differently in the various individual industries. In agriculture and cotton, wages increased more than twice as much as in the printing industry. In almost all industries wages were below the level attained at the end of the century; only in textiles as a whole were they higher in the middle of the seventies than at the end of the century. Mining wages, after the general fall in the second half of the seventies, remained on a very low level almost up to the close of the century, while wages in the printing industry showed only a slight change after the middle of the seventies, having by then almost reached the 1900 level, and having escaped the general downward movement at the end of the seventies. But though the movement has been a somewhat varied one in the individual industries and from decade to decade, on the whole one may establish a general upward trend of money wages.

But the development of money wages alone is not decisive in the development of the purchasing power of the worker, even if, as is the case in the above table, the wage data take into account changes in the number of hours worked per day. There is the very important question of wage losses through unemployment

* Wages by individual years, see Appendix to Chapter II, 1850 to 1900.

and short time, the item of variation in the cost of living, and the loss of certain sources of family income (child labour, garden plots, etc.). In the following table we give average money wages with and without taking into account losses through unemployment (unfortunately we have no information on the extent of short-time work), an index of the cost of living and an index of real wages:

AVERAGE MONEY WAGES, COST OF LIVING AND REAL WAGES, 1849 TO 1903*

($1900 = 100$)

Trade Cycle	Money Wages		Cost of Living	Real Wages	
	Gross†	Net‡		Gross†	Net‡
1849–58	60	59	103	58	57
1859–68	68	67	106	64	63
1869–79	82	81	110	75	74
1880–86	83	81	101	82	79
1887–95	89	87	96	93	91
1895–1903	96	95	96	99	99

If we compare conditions in 1850 and in 1900 we find that real wages and money wages increased by almost the same amount. Also the movement from trade cycle to trade cycle of both money wages and real wages has not been very different. Both gradually reached a high point about the middle of the seventies, which was followed by a small decline and then by a slow increase lasting to the end of the nineteenth century. There have, of course, been some variations in the movement of real and money wages, due to certain price fluctuations—but on the whole one must say that, during the fifty years under review, price fluctuations were comparatively small, and therefore of relatively little influence upon the purchasing power of wages.

If we compute trade cycle averages for the whole period since 1789 we are better able to survey the development as a whole:

* Wages by individual years, see Appendix to Chapter II, 1850 to 1900.
† Without taking into account wage losses and gains through changes in short time and unemployment.
‡ Taking into account wage losses and gains through changes in unemployment.

REAL WAGES,* 1789 TO 1903

(1900 = 100)

1789–98	.. ..	58	1843–49	53
1799–1808	.. ..	50	1849–58	57
1809–18	.. ..	43	1859–68	63
1819–28	.. ..	47	1869–79	74
1820–26	.. ..	47	1880–86	80
1827–32	.. ..	48	1887–95	91
1833–42	.. ..	51	1895–1903.. ..	99

During the years 1789 to 1858 real wages move in a semi-circle, first declining and then increasing again slowly until they regain their former level. The upward movement to be observed since the twenties continues up to the end of the century. If we had better data for the years before 1789 we would probably find that not until the last third of the nineteenth century did real wages reach the level they occupied at the beginning of the "industrial revolution." It was only in the last third of the nineteenth century that the purchasing power of the workers really reached levels not attained before under industrial capitalism.

*   *   *

We have seen above how wages moved in individual industries. Another important division among the workers is that of sex. How did the movement of wages for the two sexes compare? Our data on women's wages are very poor indeed; it is not possible to give accurate data of changes from year to year. Wood† has computed some ten-year averages which we compare with our average wages for all workers:

WAGES OF WOMEN AND AVERAGE WAGES

(1890 TO 1900 = 100)

Ten-year period	Women	Average	Ten-year period	Women	Average
1820–30	58	58	1860–70	75	74
1830–40	56	57	1870–80	93	89
1840–50	58	59	1880–90	95	90
1850–60	62	65	1890–1900	100	100

* Since 1850 net real wages.

† George Henry Wood, "Factory Legislation," etc., l.c. p. 308.

There is no sufficiently definite difference in the movement of wages (taking into account the sketchiness of the computations of the wages of women) to allow us to draw any other conclusion than that, although wages of women and men did not always move equally quickly, they moved on the whole in the same direction and not very differently.

*   *   *

Another important distinction is that between the better paid workers and the mass of the very poorly paid ones; this is the distinction between what is called the "labour aristocracy" and the mass of the workers. In a former study I have made a very rough computation of the development of wages for these two groups and I arrived at the following figures :*

WAGES OF THE LABOUR ARISTOCRACY AND THE GREAT MASS
OF THE WORKERS, 1869–1903†

(*1900 = 100*)

Trade Cycle	Labour Aristocracy	Mass of the Workers
1869–79	85	92
1880–86	88	85
1887–95	91	90
1895–1903	98	95

Though the figures are very rough and though even the trade cycle average figures cannot be regarded as anything but approximations, the difference in the development of the wages of the labour aristocracy and of the great mass of the workers is very obvious. While, in the third part of the century under review, the wages of the labour aristocracy show an increase from trade cycle to cycle, rising on the whole by more than one-sixth, the wages of the great mass of the workers fluctuated, first falling rather steeply and then increasing moderately, and showing but little change over the period as a whole.

The British ruling class, deriving enormous profits from its industrial monopoly position in the world and from its vast

* Cf. Jürgen Kuczynski, "Die Entwicklung der Lage der Arbeiterschaft in Europa und Amerika 1870–1933," *Statistische Studien zur Entwicklung der Reallöhne und Relativlöhne in England, Deutschland, U.S.A., Frankreich und Belgien.*

† Wages by individual years, see Appendix to Chapter II, 1850 to 1900.

colonial empire, gave a small part of its profits to a selected group of workers in order to keep them relatively appeased, to avoid industrial unrest in the key industries, thus trying to prevent any effective mass movement by industry as a whole directed against the existence of capitalism. And many of these labour aristocrats "gaily share the feast of England's monopoly of the world market and the colonies." (Letter of Engels to Kautsky, September 2, 1882.)

The industrial monopoly position of Britain at that time was undisputed by any other capitalist country, not excepting the United States. Its political expression can be nicely observed in Britain's trade policy, the policy of *laissez-faire*, of "no tariffs," of free trade. For free trade, lack of tariffs in every country, meant, of course, unrestricted trade for a Britain which, in quality and cheapness of production, was far ahead of other countries.

The rapid expansion of colonial exploitation (accompanied by rapidly increasing profits) can best be illustrated by a few figures referring to the years immediately following the turn of the half century, when there began the new policy of exploitation, of differentiation between groups of workers and the creation of the "labour aristocracy." Thus, between 1853 and 1864 about £40,000,000 was subscribed for Indian railways. In 1857 about £80,000,000 worth of American railroad stock was held in Britain. Between 1852 and 1858 about $60,000,000 were required for building railroads and canals in Canada, and the bulk of this money came from Great Britain. In France, in each of the six years after 1851, almost £30,000,000 was spent upon rail construction. A large part of the capital came from Britain, and at the construction of the Paris and Rouen railway, among 10,000 workers employed upwards of 4,000 were British.* British investments abroad amounted by 1860 to nearly £200,000,000; ten years later they had increased fourfold, and during the following thirty years they multiplied again by four, amounting to about £3,000,000,000.

Engels writes as follows regarding the effects of British industrial monopoly upon the conditions of the working class:

"The truth is this: during the period of England's industrial

* Cf. C. K. Hobson, *The Export of Capital.*

monopoly the English working-class have, to a certain extent, shared in the benefits of the monopoly. These benefits were unequally parcelled out amongst them; the privileged minority pocketed most, but even the great mass had, at least, a temporary share now and then."*

We have now arrived at the end of our short survey of wage conditions during the second half of the nineteenth century. On the whole, real wages increased, though the level reached was probably not very much higher than that prevailing in the second half of the eighteenth century. The increase in wages was by no means uniform; in some industries the rise was more rapid than in others, in some occupations the workers forced the ruling class to give them a special increase in the rate of real wages (labour aristocracy).

*   *   *

Our material on the variation of the number of hours worked per week is very scanty and not indicative of conditions in general. The best data have been collected by the trade unions; but, of course, working conditions among trade unionists are far better than among the immense majority of the unorganized workers. According to the statistics of some important trade unions the number of hours worked per week varied as follows:

NUMBER OF HOURS WORKED PER WEEK†‡

Years	Amalgamated Society of Engineers	Amalgamated Society of Carpenters and Joiners	Friendly Society of Iron Founders
1851–59	63 to 57	—	60 to 59½
1860–69	63 to 57, 60 to 56	64 to 52, 62 to 50½	60 to 57½
1870–79	60 to 56, 54 to 51	63 to 50, 60¼ to 49½	60 to 56½, 54

For the years 1880–89 the Amalgamated Society of Engineers reports a working week of fifty-four hours which, in the following years, declined to fifty hours in some of the factories where Society members were working. The Amalgamated Society of

* *London Commonweal*, quoted in Preface, l.c. p. xvii.
† Hours of work per week by individual years, see Appendix to Chapter II, 1850 to 1900.
‡ Longest and shortest working weeks by branches within a year during each decade.

Carpenters and Joiners reports for its best factories a working week of forty-eight and a half hours in the eighties and the first years of the nineties. The Friendly Society of Iron Founders reports a working week of fifty-four to fifty-three hours in the beginning of the nineties, little different from that of the seventies. The United Society of Boiler Makers and Iron Shipbuilders reports a working week of fifty-four hours for the years 1872–89, and of fifty-three to fifty-four hours in the beginning of the nineties.

The London Society of Compositors reports a working week of sixty-three hours for 1848–65, of sixty hours for 1866–71, and one of fifty-four hours until the beginning of the nineties. The Operative Bricklayers' Society reports a working week fluctuating between fifty-eight and a half and forty hours between the end of the sixties and the end of the eighties.

From all these data the following emerges: hours of work had a tendency to decline over the whole of the second half of the nineteenth century. Among the best organized trade unionists the working day was considerably lower than among the rest of the workers—not one case of an eleven-hour day worked on all the six week-days is reported at any time—yet we know from innumerable diverse sources that, around the middle of the century, many workers had a twelve-hour day, excluding time off for meals. The number of hours worked per day, though declining over the period as a whole, did not decline rapidly, and never without the stimulus of trade union action. If in the table giving annual data* the number of hours worked seems sometimes to increase, this is not due necessarily to a deterioration of conditions but to the fact that the union secured control of working conditions in a factory which formerly, when non-unionized, worked very long hours, and that the union did not succeed at once in reducing the number of hours worked to the level of factories which had been unionized for some time. Furthermore, we must realize that the above figures are only rough approximations, that the unions probably did not make each year a fresh and comprehensive investigation into working conditions, and that some of the figures derive only from those branches reporting or from the assumption that, since nothing

* See Appendix.

had been heard to the contrary, the number of hours worked had not changed. This causes the fixity of the working day in some unions to appear greater than it actually was; on the other hand, as is the case with the carpenters and joiners, the inclusion of new branches and factories makes the fluctuations in the number of hours worked by union members appear greater than it actually was. In conclusion, taking into account other trade union material, one can perhaps say that among well organized working groups around the middle of the century the ten-hour day (excluding meal-time, of course) was quite widespread, while at the end of the century many unions had gained for their members the nine-hour day, often with a shorter working day on Saturday.

But among the great mass of the workers a considerably longer working day was quite common—many of them still working eleven and twelve hours a day exclusive ot meal-times —at the end of the nineteenth century.

During the second half of the nineteenth century real wages rose while hours of work declined. Child labour diminished and female labour declined in certain industries involving specially hard exertion. One gets the impression that working conditions quite definitely improved. The chief counter-balancing factor of this development was the constantly growing intensity of labour, probably accompanied by an increasing accident rate. Unfortunately we have no data which might enable us to measure statistically either the development of the accident rate or this increase in intensity.

*   *   *

But there are other factors in the life of the workers which must be taken into account before we can arrive at definite conclusions as to the development of general working-class conditions in Britain. A very useful approach from another angle is a short study of nutrition and health; that is, the food which the masses eat and the state of health resulting in part from diet and in part from other factors, such as housing, industrial fatigue, and so on.

The difficulty of estimating food conditions becomes obvious from this statement, by the best authorities on the subject:

"There was a tendency for the diet of the town people to improve somewhat after 1860, when the influence of rising wages and of a fall in the price of some of the staple foods began to be felt. But it is, nevertheless, true that bread remained the chief food of the poor people. In 1892 it was found that the poor children of Bethnal Green were nourished almost entirely on bread, 83 per cent having no other solid food for seventeen out of twenty-one meals in the week."*

There was some improvement—but the great masses of the poor still lived in great want. As Engels expressed it:

". . . And the condition of the working class during this period? There was a temporary improvement even for the great mass. But this improvement always was reduced to the old level by the influx of the great body of the unemployed reserve, by the constant superseding of hands by new machinery, by the immigration of the agricultural population, now, too, more and more superseded by machines. A permanent improvement can be recognized for two 'protected' sections only of the working class. Firstly, the factory hands. . . . They are undoubtedly better off than before 1848. . . . Secondly, the great Trades' Unions. . . . But as to the great mass of working people, the state of misery and insecurity in which they live now is as low as ever, if not lower."†

The very low standard of nutrition could already be noticed among the children. Breast feeding had rapidly declined during the whole of the nineteenth century.

"The nineteenth century saw a marked decline in breast-feeding for children. . . . There were many causes. An important one affecting the poorer people was the increasing employment of women in factories. It also seems probable that the hard conditions of life, particularly during the bad periods, were responsible for a great many women being unable to nourish their children naturally. In former times most of these infants would have died, but as the nineteenth century passed an increasing proportion was successfully reared by artificial means."‡

* J. C. Drummond and Anne Wilbraham, l.c. p. 393.
† L.c. pp. xiv, xv.
‡ J. C. Drummond and Anne Wilbraham, l.c. p. 444.

By "successfully" the authors mean that they did not die. And here we must point to one of the most misleading notions introduced by scientists into the history of social conditions. They investigate health conditions by examining the incidence of death. Now this interpretation is absolutely wrong. Death statistics are indicative of the relative state of life and death but not of the state of health. For, if by improved medical services or by the discovery of new curatives many people who otherwise would have died are kept alive and are even able to work under conditions of continuous poor health, one cannot call this an improved state of health. All statistics of health, therefore, which explain, for instance, that the number of deaths from illness "X" is rapidly declining and conclude from this that the state of health in respect to illness "X" is improving, are simply misleading. For, on the contrary, is not the state of health in relation to illness "X" deteriorating if, on the one hand, the number of deaths from "X" is declining but, on the other hand, the number of people affected by "X" but saved from actual death through better medicine is increasing? One must therefore be extremely careful in using such health statistics, because they really do not tell us anything about the spread of the illness, that is, of the real state of health, but only about the number of deaths resulting from the illness.

Statistics of the number of children who have died, and of those who have survived the first ten years of life, etc., do not tell us anything about the state of health of these children.* On the other hand, some data on the real state of health, which fortunately have been collected, show us that the decline of the death rate among children is often not only not indicative but absolutely misleading. Drummond and Wilbraham say, for instance, "that by 1870 it was admitted that a proportion as high as one-third of the poor children of cities such as London and Manchester were suffering from obvious rickets. It is important to remember that such estimates were based on easily recognizable symptoms, bent limbs, rickety chest, etc., and that had there been available modern methods of diagnosis by X-rays, which detect much earlier stages, and milder forms of

---

* Except, of course, when the death rate increases, for it is extremely improbable that the state of health improves while the death rate increases.

the disease, the proportion would have been far higher. . . . In some areas, such as the Clyde district, almost every child was found to be affected (in the eighties, J. K.). A map of its (the rickets disease, J. K.) distribution over the whole of England was, in fact, a map showing the density of the industrial population."*

This had not changed by the end of the century. A survey of school children in Leeds in 1902 showed that in the poorer districts no less than half had rickets, while more than 60 per cent were suffering from carious teeth.

Bad teeth was an evil from which not only the children but the whole of the population began to suffer to an increasing degree. It is true, the death rate was not affected by this illness, the official health statistics did not take note of this evil, which became more and more widespread. But nevertheless, due probably to the fact that the diet of the people living in towns tended to become poorer in bone-forming elements, toothache became an ever recurring evil.

And yet, one would think that the influence of increased real wages and reduced hours of work should have made itself felt through a general improvement of health conditions, among the adult population at least. Fortunately, we have at our disposal a very thorough Government investigation into the physical conditions of the people made at the end of the century, so that we are able to give a picture based on a wide variety of collected material. How this investigation came about is typical of conditions under capitalism. The cause of this investigation, which aroused Whitehall, was a memorandum from Sir William Taylor, Director-General of the Army Medical Service, in which he reported that the Inspector-General of Recruiting was complaining about the poor physique of the men volunteering for service in the South African War. It was becoming increasingly difficult to get soldiers who measured up to army physical standards. Now, this was really serious. The Empire had to be guarded and expanded, and, after all, neither the Inspector-General of Recruiting nor the Director-General of the Army Medical Service were alarmist Radicals. A parlia-

* L.c. p. 453.

mentary committee was therefore appointed to look into the matter.*

Major-General H. C. Borrett, Inspector-General of Recruiting, wrote in his Annual Report for 1902 as follows:†

"The one subject which causes anxiety in the future as regards recruiting is the *gradual deterioration of the physique of the working classes* (my italics, J. K.), from whom the bulk of the recruits must always be drawn."

More cautious but not in contradiction to this, are the statements of two civilians.

Charles Booth, a pioneer in the field of investigation into labour conditions, gave this evidence before the committee:‡

(Chairman): "You are the author of *Life and Labour in London*, are you not?"—"I am."

"Did your investigation produce the impression that conditions unfavourable to the health of the community were growing in intensity?"—"I think I should not use the word 'intensity'. They are growing in amount in connection with the increase of the urban conditions of life. I could not say that the conditions have been more intense, but they are more widespread."

Booth was of the opinion that living conditions of the working class had not deteriorated (neither had they improved, in his opinion), but that unfavourable conditions prevailing in some places a number of years before, had spread to many other areas. Thus, in his opinion, there was no increase in deterioration as far as those sections of the working class were concerned, which had been the worst off a number of years before; but since more and more workers had been brought down to the level of the worst-off group, average working-class living conditions had deteriorated.

The evidence of Mr. Rowntree, another pioneer in this field, runs as follows:§

(Chairman): "You are the author of the book upon the conditions of life and labour in York?"—"Yes."

* The Inter-Departmental Committee on Physical Deterioration. Its Report was published in 1904.
† Quoted in Report, vol. ii, p. 7.
‡ Report, vol. ii, p. 47.   § Report, vol. ii, p. 200.

"Therefore you have made some considerable study of the conditions of the problems which we are asked to investigate?"— "Yes, a very fair amount."

"Are you in a position to say anything on the general question as to whether the conditions that make for deteriorated physique are increasing in intensity, or otherwise?"—"I do not think that I have any scientific information on the point. I have a general opinion that the conditions are such that it must be so. There is a greater proportion of people living in towns."

Although very cautious in expressing his opinion and very candid as to the degree of scientific accuracy in the premises on which he based his opinion, Mr. Rowntree did not hesitate to assert that conditions making for physical deterioration of the working class were becoming more widespread and forceful.

Eleven years before this, another report had been published,* from which we want to quote only one statement, that by Sir R. Giffen, who was even less inclined to advocate measures of radical social reform than Mr. Booth or Mr. Rowntree:

"Your tables show, I think, that a very large proportion of the working class of the country are earning very low wages?"— "Yes; I think that really is the important impression which one gets, that although you have three-fourths of the working classes, that is, of the men, earning between £50 and £60 per annum and upwards, yet you have 25 per cent, or something like that, below the line of 20s. per week, and that is really below the line that one could consider expedient for a minimum subsistence."

Rightly and truly, J. C. Drummond and Anne Wilbraham thus sum up conditions at the end of the nineteenth century:†

"The close of Queen Victoria's reign marked the end of an epoch. Her life had seen a great Empire consolidated, vast national wealth built up and Britain's prestige raised to a level it had never before attained. What had been the cost? By most people it was counted in terms of the handful of casualties and the comparatively insignificant financial outlay on the campaigns which had opened up new lands and new trade routes, bringing

---

* Fourth Report of the Royal Commission of Labour, London 1893. *Minutes of Evidence taken before the Royal Commission on Labour, Sitting as a Whole,* p. 475.   † L.c. p. 483.

us untold riches. Few troubled to look deeper. Few realized that the country had paid and was still paying heavily for its remarkable commercial and industrial expansion in the marked deterioration of physique and health which the appalling conditions of labour had brought about. It is no exaggeration to say that the opening of the twentieth century saw malnutrition more rife in England than it had been since the great dearths of mediaeval and Tudor times."

Malnutrition more rife than ever in the period of industrial capitalism; malnutrition more rife, in spite of the fact that real wages were probably higher than ever before in the history of industrial capitalism; malnutrition more rife, in spite of the fact that working hours were fewer and leisure longer than ever before in the history of industrial capitalism; malnutrition more rife, in spite of the fact that the labour movement was better organized and more active than ever before under industrial capitalism!

At first sight it must seem almost impossible to reconcile these different tendencies. But if we realize that there were better sanitary conditions in the towns but more congestion, a shorter working day but more intensity of work, increasing real wages but food of inferior quality and value, then we can understand what had happened during the second half of the nineteenth century. While in many respects labour conditions were improved, they deteriorated in other respects, and it was these other respects which proved to be dominant.

The difference between the development of labour conditions in the periods between 1775 and 1850, and 1850 and 1900, is not that, in the first period, labour conditions deteriorated, and improved in the second. The difference is simply in the methods of increasing the exploitation of the working class; between the methods relying chiefly upon the creation of absolute surplus value (longer working days, employment of children, decreasing wages per day and week), and the methods relying chiefly upon the creation of relative surplus value (increasing intensity of work per hour, employment of highly skilled adults, decreasing wages per amount produced). Of course, both methods were employed in both periods, but in the first period one was predominant, and, in the second, the other.

A second important difference between the two periods is that, in the first, though the textile industry was dominant, the wages of textile workers—which in 1775 were relatively high as compared with those of other workers—were lowered more than those of other industries; there was a tendency to level down wages. In the second period the iron and steel industry was dominant and there was a tendency to differentiate between certain groups and the rest, to create a labour aristocracy. The time had passed when guileless people could believe that with intelligence and industry they might become successful. But another smokescreen was spread by the ruling class: by means of intelligence and good work you might at least become a labour aristocrat. And indeed, living conditions among the labour aristocrats were considerably better than among the masses of the workers. Not a small number of labour aristocrats were destined to become traitors to their class, consciously or unconsciously. That was the idea behind the "creation of a labour aristocracy," to split the workers and to try to play off a small group with key jobs in the factories and mines against the mass of the workers.

But the existence of this small group of better paid workers, better paid at the expense of the colonial people ruthlessly exploited by British capitalism, better paid partly because of the pressure exerted by the unions, must not lead us to make the serious mistake of overlooking the fact that for the great mass of the workers living conditions, as a whole, had deteriorated.

*   *   *

While insisting on the fact, and explaining it from every possible angle, that conditions among the working class in Britain, on the average, did not improve during the second half of the nineteenth century, we must not omit to mention that the British workers were better off, on the whole, than those in other countries; better off than the workers in France and Germany; and even than those in the United States, where the large amount of immigrant labour depressed the general standard considerably.

*   *   *

Before concluding this survey of labour conditions in the second period of industrial capitalism it is necessary to give at least an indication of the development of the relative position of labour. Unfortunately not enough data are available to calculate even approximately the workers' share of the national product. Certain computations have been made by Bowley and others, but they either refer to the share of the working class as a whole in the creation of national wealth, or they give average figures per head of population but not of the workers separately. Now, the share of the working class as a whole, or rather the variations in that share, are uninteresting unless at the same time one possesses figures showing whether the number of workers was increasing faster or more slowly than the population as a whole. It is a nice game, played by numerous apologists for the capitalist system, to show, for instance, that the percentage of the national income formed by wages remained almost stable for a considerable time. This, they argue, is proof of the fact that labour conditions cannot have deteriorated, at least in relation to other groups of society; and, since the national income as a whole has increased, this means that labour has shared fully in the benefits which capitalism has brought to mankind. Such apologists either do not realize, or deliberately ignore the fact, that labour is not a fixed quantity in society; that, on the contrary, there is a process of proletarianization going on, that the number of workers increases in relation to that of other groups of society. Now, if an increasing percentage of capitalist society gets a stable share in the national income this does not mean that those belonging to that group fully share in the benefits accruing to society; on the contrary, it means that, on the average, each member of this group receives a continuously declining share in the national wealth. If "labour" gets 50 per cent of the national income, and if the number of workers making up "labour" constantly grows while the number of other people in society remains stable, then labour's percentage has to increase, or its relative position in society will become worse and worse. Therefore, those few computations of the development of the relative position of labour which are available, and which do not take into account changes in the number of persons composing the working class, are valueless.

On the other hand, it is not possible to replace them by better computations, since the necessary statistical data are missing.

But it is possible at least to throw a sidelight on the problem and on some of the facts by studying the share of labour in the national industrial product. If we compare the development of industrial production and of real wages we can measure the increasing part of the national industrial product which goes either into capital accumulation, that is the production of new means of exploitation, or into the consumption of the ruling class, or into exports either for capital accumulation outside Britain or for exchange of production and consumption goods in foreign trade. The following table makes this comparison, giving real wages per worker, industrial production per head of the population and what we call the share of the worker, or his relative position, his relative wages, as well as the share of the capitalists, the latter two simply being reverse expressions of the same fact.

RELATIVE WAGES, 1859 /TO 1903

(1900 = 100)

Cycles	Industrial per capita production	Real Wages	Relative Wages	Share of Capitalists
1859–68	51	63	124	81
1869–79	66	74	111	89
1880–86	83	79	96	104
1887–95	96	91	95	105
1895–1903	105	99	94	106

The relative position of the working class deteriorated considerably during the period under review, while the share of the capitalists* increased very much indeed. The abyss between the "two nations" grew larger. The ruling class appropriated an increasing share in the national product, accumulated more and more capital, more and more means of production, that is, more and more means of further exploitation and of accumulation for yet further exploitation. At the same time, the relative spending power of the ruling class upon consumption goods

* Unfortunately this expression includes in the above table not only the capitalists but all other non-wage earning groups of society. If we had sufficient statistical data to enable us to separate the big capitalists from the rest of the non-wage earning part of the population we would see that the share of capital in the national product increased even more than the above figures indicate.

increased. The standard of living of the ruling class improved while that of the masses deteriorated; and at the same time the means in the hands of the ruling class for still further improving their standard of living and for the further exploitation of the masses of the people also multiplied.

*   *   *

It is of great interest to note that, just as the methods of exploitation and the whole character of capitalist economy underwent certain changes in the forties of the nineteenth century, so we can also observe parallel changes in the character of the labour movement. Up to the middle of the nineteenth century the labour movement might almost be termed anarchic: without solid organization, often senselessly violent (the machine wreckers) and utopian, often concentrated upon future changes of society, neglecting attention to the concrete tasks of the day in factory, field and mine, often led by well-meaning outsiders and without a solid working-class staff.

All this changed in the second half of the nineteenth century. In place of the rapidly appearing and disappearing political trade union came the solid business trade union. Utopian dreams were replaced by definite tasks which everyday life imposed upon the workers. The benevolent outsider was replaced by the workman who began as an ordinary member, attending union meetings in the evening, and who ended as a full-time paid trade union official. Violence and strikes were often deprecated, conspiracies of revolutionary character were often deemed inappropriate, while negotiations, arbitration and respectability became labels instead of libels in the labour movement.

This characterization is deliberately simplified in order to make clear the difference in the character of these two phases in the British labour movement. Tendencies of both kinds could be observed during each of the two phases. But the chief traits are, I think, given correctly. In the next few pages I shall try to present some indicative details of the character of the British labour movement in the second half of the nineteenth century.*

* Cf. the above quoted book by the Webbs from which also the quotations below are taken.

I have used the term "business trade unionism." Two facts may explain what is meant by that. In the previous decades, numerous difficulties for the labour movement had been created by adverse court decisions. These decisions were often against the law, and touched almost every aspect of trade union activity and the life of the workers, be it the formation of a trade union branch or the attempt to abolish the truck system. Occasionally the workers resorted to the employment of legal assistance and thousands of pounds would be spent in litigation. In the forties, the miners' trade unions, which at that time grew quickly, decided to engage permanently that energetic attorney and friend of labour, W. P. Roberts, as their solicitor, and paid him a yearly salary of £1,000 to fight all their cases in the courts. We see, then, that the fight in the courts had become so important a factor in the work of the trade unions (strikes being considered a necessary evil) that unions decided on the regular employment of an able solicitor, paying him a salary which was not less than that which many business firms paid their lawyers. The second fact is that in the course of the second half of the nineteenth century the trade unions became financial institutions of great importance, administering substantial funds, sometimes exceeding £100,000, designed for death or burial benefit, for unemployment and emigration aid, for strike pay and illness, old age or accident benefit. The Webbs* correctly characterize William Allan, the General Secretary of the Amalgamated Society of Engineers, as follows: "Allan aimed at transforming the 'paid agitator' into the trusted officer of a great financial corporation." And Allan was typical of many other prominent trade unionists. He was the secretary of the strongest and most influential union (just as the textile industry had had to yield in importance to the iron and steel industry, so did the leadership of the labour movement shift from the textile workers to the workers engaged in iron, steel and related industries).

The second phase of the British labour movement, the period in which labour forgot much about politics and learned much about organization, is characterized by the growth of many stable trade unions, many of which are still in existence to-day.

* L.c. p. 235.

These unions built up a staff of well-trained trade union officials recruited from the most active workers in factory and mine. These unions laid the foundation of labour education.*

We can get a rough picture of the growth of the trade union movement by the attendance statistics of the Trade Union Congresses:†

TRADE UNION CONGRESSES' ATTENDANCE

Year and Place		Trade Unions	Trades Councils
1866	Sheffield	110,436	88,938
1871	London	280,430	
1876	Newcastle	455,490	121,998
1880	Dublin	380,913	94,511
1885	Southport	500,238	131,368
1890	Liverpool	1,592,850	333,548
1895 ⎫‡		1,414,800	
1900 ⎭ ‡		1,927,361	

These figures, with the exception of the good figures for the years 1895 and 1900, give only a very rough picture of the growth of trade unionism, but they are striking enough to impose upon the reader an impression of very solid and rapid development, especially if one keeps in mind that the most important among the unions attending these congresses are, in one form or the other, still in existence to-day.

While it is true that the trade unions began to deprecate strikes and to develop into financial corporations for the benefit of their members, this does not imply that no strikes took place, and that there were no political fights at all. An interesting passage in the Webbs' book runs:§

"It would be a mistake to assume that the inertia and supineness of the 'Amalgamated' Societies‖ was a necessary result of

---

* ". . . get knowledge, and in getting knowledge you get power. . . . Let us earnestly advise you to educate; get intelligence instead of alcohol—it is sweeter and more lasting," writes the *Flint Glass Makers' Magazine*. (Quoted by the Webbs, l.c. pp. 197–98.)

† Cf. *Abstract of Labour Statistics*, 1903.

‡ Cf. *Abstract of Labour Statistics*, 1903; these figures do not refer to attendance of congresses but to the membership of all trade unions reporting to the authorities.

§ L.c. pp. 321, 322.

‖ Many trade unions called themselves "Amalgamated Societies" (J. K.).

their accumulated funds or their friendly benefits. The remarkable energy and success of the United Society of Boilermakers and Iron Shipbuilders, established in 1832, and between 1865 and 1875 rapidly increasing in membership and funds, shows that elaborate friendly benefits are not inconsistent with a strong and consistent trade policy. This quite exceptional success is, we believe, due to the fact that the Boilermakers provided an adequate salaried staff to attend to their trade affairs.* The 'district delegates' who were, between 1873 and 1889, appointed for every important district, are absolutely unconcerned with the administration of friendly benefits, and devote themselves exclusively to the work of Collective Bargaining. Unlike the general secretaries of the Engineers, Carpenters, Stonemasons, or Ironfounders, who had but one salaried assistant, Robert Knight, the able secretary of the Boilermakers, had under his orders an expert professional staff, and was accordingly able, not only to keep both employers and unruly members in check, but also successfully to adapt the union policy to the changing conditions of the industry. In short, it was not the presence of friendly benefits, but the absence of any such class of professional organizers as exists in the organizations of the Coalminers, Cotton Operatives, and Boilermakers, that created the deadlock in the administration of the great trade friendly societies."

This passage is an excellent appreciation of conditions. There were exceptions, there were large strikes, there was a certain political activity (especially concerning non-British affairs—e.g. the help Marx got from a number of trade union leaders in the First International), but the dominant picture is that of business unions whose main strength lies in a well-organized benefit system, and who, if they do engage in any political work, concentrate chiefly on special trade union affairs, such as the recognition of the right to collective bargaining and the protection of union funds. The two high points in the political life of the trade unions, therefore, were the hurrying through Parliament in 1869 of a provisional measure giving temporary protection to trade union funds, and The

* They had, of course, just like the other unions also, a salaried staff to attend to the financial administration of the funds (J. K.).

Employers and Workmen Act of 1875, which recognized the right of the trade unions to collective bargaining.

Marx and Engels have often bitterly remarked upon the "new type" of trade unionist this development created. The "bourgeois worker," the labour aristocrat, the class-changeling, all these are the bad products of the new trade unionism of the second half of the nineteenth century. Engels* says of them:

"They form an aristocracy among the working class; they have succeeded in enforcing for themselves a relatively comfortable position, and they accept it as final. They are the model working men of Messrs. Leone Levi and Giffen, and they are very nice people indeed nowadays to deal with, for any sensible capitalist in particular and for the whole capitalist class in general."

A change in the attitude of the trade unions, and in their character and the composition of their membership, came about slowly at the end of the nineteenth century. Just as the change from the first to the second period had begun to take place before the turn of the half century—that is, still during the first period—and just as this change had a parallel in changes of the economic structure of capitalism and in the methods of exploitation, so the new change, the third phase in the history of the British labour movement, goes back in its beginnings to the second phase and has a parallel in changing economic conditions. We shall deal with this third phase in the next chapter, although we can already observe it clearly in the eighties.†

* L.c. p. xv.
† Since the sparse statistics of strikes and strike activity which we have pertain only to the nineties, when the new phase in the labour movement already exerted a considerable influence upon labour activity, we are unable to conclude this chapter with more concrete statistical evidence regarding the activities of the trade unions in the fight for an improvement of the conditions of labour. As to their activity in regard to improving the lot of their members through benefits which the workers themselves contributed, a vast collection of material is available in the union records and in the Government publications, *Labour Statistics, Statistical Tables and Report on Trade Unions*, published between 1887 and 1894, which give a most detailed picture of this aspect of trade union activity.

APPENDIX TO CHAPTER II

1850 TO 1900

I. TABLES

1. WAGES IN INDIVIDUAL INDUSTRIES, 1850 TO 1900

(1900 = 100)

Year	Agri-culture	Engineering Shipbuilding	Cotton	Textiles	Building	Printing	Coal Mining
1850	48	66	48	—	58	81	—
1851	49	67	49	—	58	81	—
1852	52	68	50	—	58	81	—
1853	56	70	53	—	58	81	—
1854	64	74	53	—	61	81	—
1855	67	74	53	—	63	81	—
1856	68	74	56	—	65	81	—
1857	66	74	57	—	66	81	—
1858	65	72	57	—	66	81	—
1859	65	72	59	—	66	81	—
1860	66	72	63	—	68	81	—
1861	68	73	63	—	68	81	—
1862	68	74	63	—	68	81	—
1863	68	74	62	—	68	81	—
1864	68	75	62	—	68	81	—
1865	69	77	66	—	71	81	—
1866	70	78	72	—	75	81	—
1867	71	76	72	—	75	82	—
1868	72	76	74	—	75	82	—
1869	73	76	73	—	75	82	—
1870	76	77	76	—	76	83	—
1871	80	79	79	—	77	86	—
1872	87	83	82	—	79	86	—
1873	92	86	83	—	80	86	—
1874	96	87	84	107	84	91	89
1875	98	87	84	105	88	92	79
1876	98	87	86	105	90	93	71
1877	98	88	88	102	90	94	66
1878	96	87	82	92	88	94	62
1879	92	83	79	88	87	94	62
1880	88	84	81	90	87	94	61
1881	86	86	84	94	87	94	63
1882	86	88	84	94	87	94	68
1883	86	88	85	93	87	94	69
1884	86	87	85	94	87	94	66
1885	84	86	84	90	87	94	63
1886	84	84	83	89	87	94	61
1887	85	85	85	90	88	94	61
1888	87	88	88	94	88	94	65
1889	88	91	89	95	89	94	76

1. WAGES IN INDIVIDUAL INDUSTRIES, 1850 TO 1900—*continued*
(1900 = 100)

Year	Agri-culture	Engineering Shipbuilding	Cotton	Textiles	Building	Printing	Coal Mining
1890	90	93	90	95	90	96	86
1891	91	93	93	97	90	98	87
1892	92	92	95	96	91	98	79
1893	92	91	94	95	92	99	80
1894	93	91	94	95	93	99	76
1895	92	91	94	95	94	99	73
1896	92	94	95	95	95	99	72
1897	93	96	96	95	96	99	73
1898	95	98	96	95	98	99	79
1899	96	100	98	98	99	99	84
1900	100	100	100	100	100	100	100

2. MONEY WAGES, COST OF LIVING AND REAL WAGES
1850 TO 1900
(1900 = 100)

Year	Money Wages Gross*	Money Wages Net†	Cost of Living	Real Wages Gross*	Real Wages Net†
1850	56	55	94	60	59
1851	56	55	92	61	60
1852	56	54	92	61	59
1853	62	62	99	62	63
1854	64	64	112	57	57
1855	65	63	115	56	55
1856	65	64	115	57	56
1857	62	60	110	57	55
1858	62	56	102	60	55
1859	62	62	101	62	61
1860	64	64	105	61	62
1861	64	62	108	59	58
1862	65	61	105	62	58
1863	66	64	102	64	62
1864	69	70	101	68	69
1865	71	71	103	69	69
1866	74	73	109	68	68
1867	73	70	114	64	61
1868	73	69	112	65	61
1869	73	70	109	67	64
1870	75	74	109	69	68
1871	77	78	109	71	72
1872	82	83	114	71	73
1873	87	88	116	75	76
1874	87	88	113	77	78
1875	86	87	109	79	79
1876	85	85	108	79	79
1877	85	83	110	77	76
1878	83	79	108	76	73
1879	82	75	103	79	72

2. MONEY WAGES, COST OF LIVING AND REAL WAGES
1850 TO 1900—*continued*

(*1900 = 100*)

Year	Money Wages		Cost of Living	Real Wages	
	Gross*	Net†		Gross*	Net†
1880	82	80	106	77	75
1881	82	82	105	78	78
1882	82	83	106	78	78
1883	83	84	104	80	81
1884	84	80	102	82	78
1885	84	78	90	93	87
1886	83	77	96	86	79
1887	84	79	94	89	84
1888	85	83	94	90	88
1889	87	88	97	90	91
1890	91	92	97	94	95
1891	91	91	98	93	93
1892	90	88	98	93	90
1893	93	86	96	97	90
1894	90	87	94	96	92
1895	90	88	93	98	95
1896	91	91	92	99	99
1897	93	92	94	98	98
1898	94	94	96	98	98
1899	96	97	95	101	102
1900	100	100	100	100	100

WAGES OF THE LABOUR ARISTOCRACY AND THE GREAT MASS OF THE WORKERS, 1869–1900

Year	Gross Money Wages		Unemployment	
	Labour Aristocracy	Great Mass	Labour Aristocracy	Great Mass
	1900 = 100		Per cent.	Per cent.
1869	78	82	6·3	6·0
1870	79	85	4·1	3·8
1871	79	87	1·9	1.6
1872	81	94	1·1	0·9
1873	84	100	1·2	1·2
1874	88	99	1·6	1·7
1875	88	97	2·1	2·4
1876	90	96	3·0	3·7
1877	91	94	3·8	4·7
1878	90	90	6·3	6·8
1879	89	83	11·8	11·4

* Without taking into account wage losses and gains through changes in short-time and unemployment.

† Taking into account changes in unemployment.

WAGES OF THE LABOUR ARISTOCRACY AND THE GREAT MASS OF THE WORKERS, 1869-1900—continued

| | Gross Money Wages | | Unemployment | |
| Year | Labour Aristocracy | Great Mass | Labour Aristocracy | Great Mass |
	1900 = 100		Per cent.	Per cent.
1880	88	84	6·4	5·5
1881	89	86	4·5	3·5
1882	89	87	2·9	2·3
1883	89	87	3·2	2·6
1884	88	85	7·8	8·1
1885	88	83	10·0	9·3
1886	88	82	10·9	10·2
1887	89	82	8·5	7·6
1888	89	85	5·9	4·9
1889	90	91	2·7	2·1
1890	91	93	2·2	2·1
1891	92	95	3·0	3·5
1892	92	92	5·4	6·3
1893	92	92	7·3	7·5
1894	92	91	7·8	6·9
1895	93	91	6·3	5·8
1896	95	91	2·8	3·3
1897	96	92	3·0	3·3
1898	98	93	2·5	2·8
1899	99	96	1·8	2·0
1900	100	100	2·6	2·5

NUMBER OF HOURS WORKED PER WEEK*

Year	Amalgamated Society of Engineers	Amalgamated Society of Carpenters and Joiners	Friendly Society of Iron Founders
1851	63 to 57	—	60 to 59½
1852	63 to 57	—	60 to 59½
1853	63 to 56	—	60 to 59½
1854	63 to 57	—	60 to 59½
1855	63 to 57	—	60 to 59½
1856	63 to 57	—	60 to 59½
1857	63 to 57	—	60 to 59½
1858	63 to 57	—	60 to 59½
1859	63 to 57	—	60 to 59½
1860	63 to 57	—	60 to 57½
1861	63 to 57	—	60 to 57½
1862	63 to 56	—	60 to 57½
1863	63 to 56	—	60 to 57½
1864	63 to 56	64 to 52	60 to 57½
1865	63 to 56	63 to 50½	60 to 57½
1866	60 to 56	63 to 50	60 to 57½
1867	60 to 56	63½ to 50½	60 to 57½
1868	60 to 56	62 to 50½	60 to 57½
1869	60 to 56	63½ to 50½	60 to 57½

* Cf. *Labour Statistics, Statistical Tables and Report on Trade Unions*, C. 5104, 1887, and the following years.

NUMBER OF HOURS WORKED PER WEEK*—*continued*

Year	Amalgamated Society of of Engineers	Amalgamated Society of Carpenters and Joiners	Friendly Society of Iron Founders
1870	60 to 56	61¾ to 50½	60 to 56½
1871	60 to 54	63 to 50	60 to 56½
1872	54 to 51	61¾ to 50	60 to 56½
1873	54 to 51	60¾ to 49½	58½ to 54
1874	54 to 51	62 to 49	54
1875	54 to 51	62 to 49	54
1876	54 to 51	63 to 48½	54
1877	54 to 51	64 to 48½	54
1878	54 to 51	63 to 48½	54
1879	54	63 to 48½	54

II. Sources and Remarks

For the statistics of wages in individual industries compare the studies of A. L. Bowley and G. H. Wood, "The Statistics of Wages in the United Kingdom during the last Hundred Years," in the *Journal of the Royal Statistical Society*, 1899–1910; A. L. Bowley, *Wages in the United Kingdom in the Nineteenth Century*, and *Wages and Income in the United Kingdom since 1860*, Cambridge, 1937; the regular retrospective statistics in the pre- 1914–18 war issues of the *Abstract of Labour Statistics of the United Kingdom;* and *Returns of Wages, Published between 1830 and 1886*, London 1887. Statistics of wages for all industries are taken from G. H. Wood's article "Real Wages and the Standard of Comfort since 1850," *Journal of the Royal Statistical Society*, 1909.

The cost of living data are based on those given by Wood (*Real Wages and the Standard of Comfort*); while Wood, however, takes into account only half the increase in rents because, he argues, accommodation improved too, I have used his figures for the total increase in rents. From an article by H. W. Singer, "An Index of Urban Land Rents and House Rents in England and Wales, 1845–1913," *Econometrica*, Vol. 9, No. 324, July–October 1941, one may perhaps draw the conclusion that rents have increased even more than I assumed.

Professor Bowley recently computed a cost of living index, also a very rough one, and it is perhaps interesting to compare the development of the cost of living according to the original index of Wood with his index as corrected by me, and then with the new Bowley index (for the latter cf. *Wages and Income in the United Kingdom since* 1860):

* Cf. *Labour Statistics, Statistical Tables and Report on Trade Unions*, C. 5104, 1887, and the following years.

COST OF LIVING

Year	Wood	Wood-Kuczynski	Bowley
1850–54	100	100	100
1860–64	105	106	113
1870–74	111	114	115
1880	105	108	104
1890	94	99	88
1900	94	102	90

The second index is that used in this book. None of the three indices is of really good quality. Each has a definite bias in showing the development of the cost of living as too favourable for the worker. Wood argues that housing improved in the course of time, and, therefore, that the entire increase in rents should not be included in the cost-of-living index. But this argument does not seem logical. The worker always lives in the worst rooms available. If this accommodation improves in the course of time—that is, if the worst rooms in 1940 are better than the worst rooms in 1840, and if the rent is correspondingly higher—one cannot argue that, if rooms such as were inhabited by workers in 1840 still existed to-day, the worker would get them more cheaply than those in which he now lives. For the rooms of 1840 do not exist, and one cannot include in a cost-of-living index prices of goods which cannot be obtained. On the other hand, and this factor counts for much in the worker's budget, the quality of clothing has undoubtedly become inferior to that of forty and a hundred years ago, and this deterioration has necessarily led to a more frequent renewal of the worker's "wardrobe." The shorter expectation of life of socks and other clothing has not been taken into account in the cost-of-living index. The higher and still mounting fares the worker has to pay in order to reach his place of work, and the fact that, with the disappearance of garden plots, the worker has to pay for goods which he once did not need to buy, are also not taken into account. All this leads to too small an increase, or too large a decrease, in the cost-of-living index and, therefore, to a bias unfavourable to the workers.

On the other hand, the wage index also shows a development too favourable to the workers. All the advantages gained through trade union action in the cities and large towns and in the bigger concerns, are faithfully reflected by the index, while the lagging behind of conditions in small firms and in smaller towns find only inadequate reflection in the wage index. Furthermore, the growth of short-time work finds no expression at all in our figures, since no data on this subject are available. The growing introduction of piece rates in the place of time rates works in the other direction, but this trend is overcompensated by the above-mentioned factors and those which follow. First, the trend from skilled to unskilled work, the dilution of labour which proceeded throughout the whole period, finds no expression in our wage index; second, no data on salaried employees are included and their conditions have deteriorated over the whole period. Seventy years ago a salaried worker belonged, socially and financially, to an absolutely different group from that of the wage-workers; to-day many "black-coat" workers are paid less than some wage-workers.

Finally, we must not forget the following interesting development: average wages tend to show an increase greater than that of wages paid in individual industries because, during the second half of the nineteenth century, there was a movement from lower paying to higher paying industries, chiefly from the textile to the iron, steel and metal industries. Of course, the number of workers in the textile and clothing industries also increased, but that in the iron and steel and other industries increased at a much greater rate. Even had real wages in each individual industry remained stable, average real wages would have increased because a larger number of workers were working in the higher paying industries. The not inconsiderable influence of this factor can be seen from the following table, which gives, according to Wood (cf. *Real Wages and the Standard of Comfort since 1850*), average wages with and without taking into account the relative increase in the number of workers in different industries:

AVERAGE WAGES IN ENGLAND
(RECALCULATED ON BASIS 1900 = 100)

Year	Without taking into account relative number of workers	With
1850	66	56
1860	72	64
1870	81	75
1880	86	82
1890	93	91
1900	100	100

The more rapid increase of the average which takes into account the relative changes in the number of workers in the individual industries, is quite obvious.

As we have seen, both the index of the cost of living as well as the index of wages tend to convey the impression of a more favourable development of labour conditions than has actually taken place. Therefore, one must always deduct something if real wages are moving up; one must assume that they are actually declining if they seem to be stable, and that when they do show a decline the fall has actually been steeper than the figures indicate.

The only data available for the study of unemployment are the records of the trade unions which, up to the eighties, refer chiefly to skilled workers or to workers in a restricted number of industries. The easiest accessible source for unemployment data for the years up to 1870 is Wood's above-mentioned study *Real Wages and the Standard of Comfort since 1850*. For later years see the *Abstract of Labour Statistics*.

UNEMPLOYMENT, 1850 TO 1900

Year	Percentage	Year	Percentage	Year	Percentage	Year	Percentage
1850	4.0	1863	6.0	1876	3.7	1889	2.1
1851	3.9	1864	2.7	1877	4.7		
1852	6.0	1865	2.1	1878	6.8	1890	2.1
1853	1.7	1866	3.3	1879	11.4	1891	3.5
1854	2.9	1867	7.4			1892	6.3
1855	5.4	1868	7.9	1880	5.5	1893	7.5
1856	4.7	1869	6.7	1881	3.5	1894	6.9
1857	6.0			1882	2.3	1895	5.8
1858	11.9			1883	2.6	1896	3.3
1859	3.8	1870	3.9	1884	8.1	1897	3.3
		1871	1.6	1885	9.3	1989	2.8
1860	1.9	1872	0.9	1886	10.2	1899	2.0
1861	5.2	1873	1.2	1887	7.6		
1862	8.4	1874	1.7	1888	4.9	1900	2.5
		1875	2.4				

As to relative wages, the relative position of the worker, see for a detailed description of the underlying principles Vol. VII of this work and, until this is published, my book on *Labour Conditions in Western Europe 1820 to 1935*, London 1937, pp. 26–29. The index of the physical volume of production has been "treated" by multiplying it by the result of a division of the wholesale price index into the cost-of-living index, in order to adjust the character of the index of the physical volume to that of a real wage index.* The figures used for this treatment and those treated are:

(*1900 = 100*)

Cycles	Physical Volume of Industrial Production	Wholesale Prices	Retail Prices
1859–68	46	133	106
1869–79	62	129	110
1880–86	74	106	101
1887–95	83	91	96
1895–1903	97	89	96

For production figures we used the above-mentioned index by W. Hoffmann, for wholesale prices that of Sauerbeck and the *Statist*, for retail prices the Wood-Kuczynski cost-of-living index, for population data the official statistics, and for real wages our real wage index. The figures, of course, are only rough approximations. We, therefore, have not given relative wages by years, but only by trade-cycle averages. All the errors contained in the real wage index may have been multiplied by errors in the "treated" index of industrial per capita production. The only really reliable index is that of the population. The index of industrial production probably has a slight tendency to increase too quickly because of the omission from it of some important consumption goods industries. This slight tendency becomes a definite bias through the omission of agricultural production, which really should be included in order that the index become one of national production.

The wholesale price index probably suffers seriously from the omission of prices of most finished products. Neither for Britain nor for any other country does a satisfactory wholesale price index exist because average prices of finished manufactured goods are almost unknown and, therefore, are not taken into account. It is furthermore not advisable simply to replace a retail price index including the prices of all goods by a cost-of-living index including only the prices of such goods which the Government regards as necessities in a worker's household.

* An argument against this procedure can be found in a review by A. L. Bowley in the *Journal of the Royal Statistical Society*, 1937.

Unfortunately, just as there is no index of agricultural production, so is there no comprehensive retail price index.

The publication of our figures of relative wages is justified only because they show such a definite downward trend that there can be no doubt, notwithstanding all possible errors, that relative wages have declined considerably in the course of the period reviewed here. Unfortunately, I have here to repeat a wish, expressed whenever I have published figures on relative wages: that my own computations may soon be superseded by those of others on the basis of new research on this really important subject. But, up to now, nobody, with the exception of one or two research workers in the Brookings Institution in Washington and in the Labor Research Association in New York, has undertaken any serious study in this direction.

On the history of the labour movement see also the study by Allen Hutt, *British Trade Unionism*.

CHAPTER III

1900 TO THE PRESENT DAY

IMPERIALISM, finance capitalism, monopoly capitalism, wars and revolutions, decay and parasitism—all these are characteristics of the third period of capitalism which began about the end of the last century and which, unfortunately, survives in most countries.

A new period of capitalism means also a new period in the development of the labour movement and in the evolution and methods of exploitation; it means a new period in the history of labour conditions.

During the first period, which began with the industrial revolution and ended somewhere around the middle of the last century, industrial capitalism was in its infancy, the labour movement was rather unstable and not very successful, and the capitalists concentrated to a large extent upon the creation of absolute surplus value. During the second period industrial capitalism reached full maturity, extending all over the world and becoming a formidable power; the labour movement became a well-organized force though comprising only a relatively small part of the working class; capitalism became more "refined" in its methods of exploitation and concentrated chiefly upon the creation of relative surplus value. During the first period, labour conditions deteriorated almost everywhere. During the second period, certain groups of workers—the skilled and well-organized workers, the labour aristocracy—experienced an improvement of working and living conditions, while the great mass of the workers experienced a deterioration of living conditions.

During the third period, which is under review in the following pages, capitalism in Britain entered a period of partially retarded growth. The production of means of production developed as follows:*

* Cf. Jürgen Kuczynski; *Weltproduktion und Welthandel in den letzten 100 Jahren.*

PRODUCTION OF MEANS OF PRODUCTION

(1909–14 = 100)

Trade Cycle	Index	Rate of Growth per cent
1869–79	46	—
1880–86	57	25
1887–95	66	16
1895–1903	79	20
1904–08	91	15
1909–14	100	10
1915–23	94	6 (decline)
1924–32	105	12
1909–14 to 1924–32	—	5

At the same time Britain's foreign trade showed similar tendencies:*

FOREIGN TRADE (VOLUME)

(1909–14 = 100)

Trade Cycle	Index	Rate of Growth per cent
1869–79	41	
1880–86	55	34
1887–95	67	22
1895–1903	79	18
1904–08	89	13
1909–14	100	12
1915–23	87	13 (decline)
1924–32	107	23
1909–14 to 1924–32	—	7

We have entered the period of which Engels anxiously asks:†
"And the working class? If, even under the unparalleled commercial and industrial expansion, from 1848 to 1866, they have to undergo such misery . . . what will it be when this dazzling period is brought finally to a close; when the present dreary stagnation shall not only become intensified, but this, its intensified condition, shall become the permanent and normal state of English trade?"

True, there has been no absolute stagnation, but progress slowed down greatly. True, during this period, world industrial capitalism developed rapidly, world production and world

* Cf. Jürgen Kuczynski: *Weltproduktion und Welthandel in den letzten 100 Jahren.*
† L.c. p. xvii.

trade were still increasing considerably; but in the old capitalist countries, and especially in Great Britain, the oldest, development came almost to a standstill: production between 1924 and 1932, the last full trade cycle preceding the present world war, was barely higher than that of twenty years before, in spite of the fact that the number of people living in Great Britain had not inconsiderably increased; per capita production of industrial means of production has, in fact, declined; and foreign trade —reckoned in relation to the size of the population—has declined too.

But capitalism was still developing in Britain, too, during the period under review. It was transforming itself into monopoly-capitalism. Industrial capital was merging with bank capital into a unity called finance capital. Foreign capital holdings continued to increase. New colonies, new domains of exploitation, were added to those already within the Empire. The first world war was won and Britain's share in the spoils was no small one. Germany, Britain's chief industrial competitor in Europe, was beaten and her colonial empire smashed. All this occurred within a few decades; and yet this change in the character of British capitalism—a change which took place in other countries also—this apparently improved organization and competitive position of British capitalism could not counterbalance its tendencies of decay and degradation.

Furthermore, once German industry and commerce—Britain's chief competitors from 1890 to 1914—appeared to have been eliminated from the world market, the United States emerged as Britain's chief and much more powerful rival. After some years, Germany began to reappear on the world market. Furthermore, in the East the birth of the Soviet Union had eliminated one of the most profitable fields of investment. Finally, in recent years, one war after the other, beginning with the occupation of Manchuria by Japan, upset world conditions. Fascism spread. In 1939, in consequence of the policy of the ruling classes in the foremost capitalist countries, the second world war broke out. To-day, the greatest effort by all peoples is needed to beat down the terrible menace of German fascism.

*   *   *

The tendencies of stagnation and retrogression are very clear from the tables on production and foreign trade. On the following pages we shall study the tendencies of decay and parasitism, so intimately connected with imperialism, with finance capitalism. Some years ago I endeavoured to examine these phenomena with regard to the United States* and calculated an index of unproductivity in that country. I shall now try to do the same for Britain.

There are three factors which enter into this index of unproductivity. The first one is the decreasing use made of the labour force available, creating increased unemployment. The second factor is the increasing number of salaried persons engaged in occupations which under Socialism would either become superfluous or would shrink to reasonable proportions—such as banking, private insurance, etc.; we have measured the growth of this element of decay by computing the percentage by which the number of all non-working class occupied persons, excluding farmers, has grown in proportion to that of the workers. The third factor is the high percentage of the national productive power engaged in the production of armaments; I have measured this factor by calculating the percentage of the national income allocated to military expenditure.

AN INDEX OF UNPRODUCTIVITY, 1880 TO 1939†

(1880 = 100)

I. Inroads in Labour Force through Unemployment, Over-Employment of Unproductive Forces, and Armament Expenditure as percentage of National Income

Trade Cycle	Inroads in Labour Force through Unemployment (Full Labour Force equal 100)	Inroads in Labour Force through Unemployment and Over-employment of Unproductive Forces	Percentage of National Income spent on Armaments
1880–86	94·1	93	2·6
1887–95	94·8	93	2·4
1895–1903	96·5	93	4·4
1904–08	94·8	90	3·5
1909–14	96·0	88	6·1
1915–23	94·4	86	25·0
1924–32	87·1	77	2·5
1933–39	85·9	75	5·9

* Cf. *New Fashions in Wage Theory*, London 1937, p. 72 f.

† Figures for individual years, see Appendix to Chapter III, 1900 to the Present Day.

II. UNPRODUCTIVITY, 1880 TO 1939*

(1880 = 100)

Trade Cycle	Index
1880–86	101
1887–95	102
1895–1903	104
1904–08	107
1909–14	111
1915–23	157
1924–32	123
1933–39	130

During the earlier trade cycles under review unproductivity increased continuously from cycle to cycle. During the last cycle, before the first world war, unproductivity was about 10 per cent higher than in the beginning of the eighties. During the war unproductivity, of course, rose steeply. After the war it declined—yet it remained considerably higher than before the first world war. During the last trade cycle it rose again, only slightly influenced by the high figure for 1939, the first year of the new world war.

*   *   *

How did the workers fare in this period? Did conditions eventually improve generally? Did they continue to deteriorate? And, if so, were all workers affected, as during the first period of industrial capitalism, or were certain groups excepted as during the second period of industrial capitalism? Did the distribution of a small share in the extra profits from colonial exploitation affect a larger number of workers, or did monopoly-capitalism decide to swallow the whole share? Did the methods of exploitation change and to what extent? Is there a third method of obtaining surplus value besides the creation of absolute and relative surplus value? Did real wages continue to increase while other conditions affecting the labour and living conditions

---

* Figures for individual years, see Appendix to Chapter III, 1900 to the Present Day.

of the working class deteriorated, or was there more uniformity in the development of the various aspects of the worker's life?

An examination of the following tables gives a clear answer to these questions. We begin with a study of the development of wages. The following table gives a survey of the development of wage rates in the five most important industries of the country.

WAGES RATES IN INDIVIDUAL INDUSTRIES, 1904 TO 1939*

(1900 = 100)

Trade Cycle	Building	Coal Mining	Engineering	Textiles	Agriculture
1904–08	100	87	101	105	103
1909–14	103	94	104	109	108
1915–23	192	166	195	188	—
1924–32	207	130	179	189	197
1933–39	203	129	188	175	206

If we compare the wages at the beginning of the century with those of the thirties, we notice that one industry has developed differently from the others: wages in the coal industry are only about 30 per cent higher than in 1900, while wages in other industries have increased 100 per cent or more; and even in the constantly depressed textile industries they have increased by 75 per cent.

Up to the first world war, only the coal industry showed sharp downward breaks, though when the war started the coal industry was again paying wages which had not changed very much more than those of other industries, being about 10 per cent below the average index. By the end of the war, the coal industry had moved up to about the average level, while engineering (armament industries) and agriculture (in an attempt to keep the workers on the land) had increased above the average. In the years following the war, the coal and engineering industries suffered the severest set-back, while in .the thirties the textile industries were prominently sagging.

The following table enables us to survey general conditions and also to take into account the movement of prices.

* Wages in individual years, see Appendix to Chapter III, 1900 to the Present Day.

AVERAGE MONEY WAGES, COST OF LIVING AND REAL WAGES,
1904 TO 1939*

(1900 = 100)

Trade Cycle	Money Wages Gross	Money Wages Net	Cost of Living	Net Real Wages Per Full Time Week	Net Real Wages Per Unemployed and Employed Worker
1904–08	100	97	102	97	95
1909–14†	104	101	108	95	93
1915–23	188	180	204	89	87
1924–32	186	164	181	98	91
1933–39†	185	163	169	104	96

This last table is perhaps the clearest and most impressive. It shows that up to the 1914–18 war real wages had a tendency to decline, that the post-war increase was very small, and that there was not a single trade cycle during which real wages reached the level of the turn of the century. If we except the early decades of the first period of industrial capitalism we find that for the first time real wages had a definite downward trend. Beginning and end of industrial capitalism, childhood and senility, unbalanced but vigorous growth and weak decay, produce the same phenomenon: declining real wages, declining purchasing power of the masses of the people. The methods of exploitation become similar. In both periods the rate of exploitation is increased by a definite lowering of the wage standard.

*   *   *

This lowering of the wage standard, of the purchasing power of the working class, occurs not only among the great mass of the workers, but also among the so-called labour aristocracy; one can even say that the standard of purchasing power of the labour aristocracy is declining at a somewhat quicker rate than that of the great mass of the workers.‡

   * Wages for individual years, see Appendix to Chapter III, 1900 to the Present Day. The general index includes many more industries than are included in the preceding table.
   † Incomplete cycles; crisis and depression years missing, cycles being interrupted by war.
   ‡ Cf. my above-mentioned study, *Die Entwicklung der Lage der Arbeiterschaft in Europa und Amerika, 1870–1933.*

NET REAL WAGES OF THE GREAT MASS OF THE WORKERS AND OF THE LABOUR ARISTOCRACY

(1895–1903 = 100)

Trade Cycle	Labour Aristocracy	Great Mass
1895–1903	100	100
1904–08	93	97
1909–14	92	96
1924–32	91	95

The real wages of the labour aristocracy had about twice as strong a downward trend as had those of the great mass of the workers, but the purchasing power of the labour aristocracy, as composed in the nineteenth century, still remained higher in spite of the steeper decline. The effects of monopoly capitalism with all its tendencies to decay—of imperialism as the period in which the world has been divided up and new markets and raw material sources usually have to be acquired through costly wars —the effects of the end of Britain's world monopoly as the out-standing industrial power, the policy of giving to a section of the working class increasing benefits from the extra profits accruing from the colonial empire. What Engels prophesied has come true:[*]

". . . With the breakdown of that monopoly, the English working class will lose that privileged position; it will find itself generally—the privileged and leading minority not excepted— on a level with its fellow-workers abroad."[†]

[*] L.c. pp. xvii, xviii.

[†] That does not mean that the labour aristocracy is disappearing completely or that the standard of living of the whole of the labour aristocracy is declining. If we look closer we find the following development: the labour aristocracy becomes smaller in numbers and the smaller number is farther removed from the standard of living of the working class than before If one could construct an index of the real income of the labour aristocracy taking into account the fact that the number of people (it is difficult to say: number of workers) belonging to it becomes smaller and smaller then one would find that the position of the labour aristocracy has improved during the twentieth century.

While during the nineteenth century the labour aristocracy was composed of a not inconsiderable number of skilled workers, it consists to-day chiefly of former workers who have gained positions (or who have been given positions by the State) in the trade union and co-operative bureaucracy, in Parliament, on all sorts of committees, municipal offices, State offices, etc. They all have so-called soft jobs and safe jobs, and their standard of living and interests are often opposed to those of the workers. The labour aristocracy in its nineteenth century composition is disappearing. The institution of the labour aristocracy as safe-guard for the ruling classes has been maintained—at considerably smaller cost.

The above wage figures indicate fairly clearly the changes in the purchasing power of the worker. But they do not indicate how the worker actually lives. They show that he can buy less to-day than ten years ago—but they do not show whether the worker can buy enough to-day.

During the twentieth century a number of studies have been made on the subject: what must the worker be able to buy in order to reproduce his working power daily and reproduce himself—that is, to raise a family? One of the most recent studies on "the necessities of physical fitness for themselves (the workers, J. K.) and those dependent on them" is that by Mr. Seebohm Rowntree.* On the basis of the computations of Mr. Rowntree of what a worker needs, I have computed a table showing the percentage of workers who earn less than Rowntree's minimum necessary to buy "the necessities of physical fitness."† These figures refer to the last pre-war years; at the end of 1939 conditions were already worse, and to-day they have further deteriorated.

PERCENTAGE OF WORKERS WHO EARNED LESS THAN THE ROWNTREE MINIMUM‡ DURING THE YEARS BEFORE THE WAR

Industry	Male Workers per cent	Female Workers per cent	All Workers per cent
Mining, other than coal-mining and quarrying	75	75	75
Treatment of non-metalliferous mine and quarry products	10	80	11
Brick, pottery, glass, chemical products, etc.	4	70	16
Metal, engineering, shipbuilding, etc.	5	55	11
Textiles	40	50	46
Leather	12	65	24
Clothing	12	35	29
Food, drink, tobacco	7	35	18
Woodworking	6	25	8
Paper, printing, stationery, etc. ..	1	15	5
Transport and storage (other than railways)	3	35	4
Public utility services	55	88	57
Coal mining	80	—	80
Building	50	—	50
Railways	25	—	25
Agriculture	100	100	100

* B. S. Rowntree, *The Human Needs of Labour*, London, 1937.
† Cf. J. Kuczynski, *Hunger and Work*, London, 1938, p. 107.
‡ The Rowntree Minimum for a working-class family, the husband not doing specially heavy work, the family including three children, was before the war about 55s.

If we apply these percentages to the number of workers engaged in industry and agriculture, we find that about four million adult male workers earn less than the Rowntree minimum of existence and physical fitness for a family of five (including three children) ; and that about two million adult female workers earn less than the Rowntree minimum for a woman living without dependants. If we exclude from these all the workers who have no family or a smaller one, and married women, and if we include those workers who earn the minimum for a family of three children but who have larger families than this, as well as all the women with somebody dependent upon them, we arrive for 1937, at a rough calculation, at the figure of about ten million working men, women and children who are living under such conditions that they cannot even keep fit for work or grow up fit for work; they are not able to recuperate completely from the exhausting work they are doing, and thus have to expend more energy than they can replace.

Ten million working men, women and children underfed, underclothed, badly housed at a time which was "generally regarded as prosperous"; at a time which was rightly regarded as one of record employment and, as post-war 1914–18 conditions go, of comparatively little unemployment! This certainly is indicative of labour conditions in the period of monopolism, of imperialism, of capitalism in decay.

These figures are strikingly supported by the foremost British authority on food problems, Sir John Orr, who writes :*

"The diet of nearly a third of the population is still not up to the standard which we now know to be necessary for health."

And comparing conditions in Britain with those in other countries he remarks :†

"The proportion of the population falling below the standard is no greater in Great Britain than it is in any of the other great nations, though it is probably greater than in some of the smaller democracies."

But food is only one of the things necessary to life which the workers cannot buy in sufficient quantities. Others are clothing, medical services, educational facilities, etc. Often the worker has

* Sir John Orr and David Lubbock, *Feeding the People in War-Time*, London, 1940, p. 1.   † L.c. p. 31.

to choose between an adequate diet or being housed in decent conditions or clothing his family sufficiently. One of the most striking examples of the effect of living on a decent level in one of these respects upon other aspects of the workers' life are the experiences of the medical officer of health of Stockton-on-Tees, Dr. M'Gonigle.* He investigated health conditions among workers who had been taken from overcrowded and insanitary houses and had been moved to a new and decent council estate. The effect of this re-housing was, curiously enough, not an improvement but a deterioration in health conditions. The reason for this surprising result was that, while the workers were considerably better housed, this better housing was so expensive that they had to cut down their food budget severely. This reduction in food expenditure had such grave effect upon their general standard of health that it more than cancelled out the benefits of better housing.

This is one of the clearest examples of the tragic conditions under which one-third of the British people lived before the present war: if they wanted decent housing conditions, they had to forego sufficient nourishment, or the reverse; if they wanted adequate food, they had to clothe themselves inadequately, and so on. One-third of the people, at least, but probably more, had to live at a standard which in the end must lead to degeneration.

*   *   *

In describing conditions in the forties and earlier, Engels points out, and quotes Carlyle to the same effect, that one of the most degrading elements in the life of the workers was extreme insecurity. Periods of increasing business activity and scarcity of labour are followed by others of crisis and unemployment. This insecurity in the life of the workers may also be noted during the second half of the nineteenth century, up to the first world war. Since then—that is, during the last twenty years—an additional factor has still further worsened conditions and intensified insecurity; while during a period of crisis unemployment increases rapidly, during the periods of growing trade activity unemployment does decline but never so much that there is a labour scarcity. On the contrary, even

* *Poverty and Public Health*, by G. C. M. M'Gonigle and J. Kirby.

during periods of considerably augmented trade, there remains a vast army of unemployed.

The change can be clearly observed in the following table:

PERCENTAGE UNEMPLOYED, 1900 TO 1939

Year	Percentage	Year	Percentage	Year	Percentage	Year	Percentage
1900	2·5	1910	4·7	1920	2·4	1930	15·8
1901	3·3	1911	3·0	1921	16·6	1931	21·1
1902	4·0	1912	3·2	1922	14·1	1932	21·9
1903	4·7	1913	2·1	1923	11·6	1933	19·8
1904	6·0	1914	3·3	1924	10·2	1934	16·6
1905	5·0	1915	1·1	1925	11·0	1935	15·3
1906	3·6	1916	0·4	1926	12·3	1936	12·9
1907	3·7	1917	0·7	1927	9·6	1937	10·6
1908	7·8	1918	0·8	1928	10·7	1938	12·5
1909	7·7	1919	2·4	1929	10·3	1939	10·3

Unemployment was "normal" during the years preceding the beginning of the first world war. During the war, unemployment declined considerably, many workers being called up and others compelled to produce to the utmost of their ability. During 1919 and 1920 unemployment remained low, then during the crisis of 1921 it rose rapidly, but probably was no higher than during other severe crises. After the crisis, however, unemployment did not fall to "normal," but remained on a high level until the new crisis in 1930 drove unemployment far above the 1921 crisis level. For about three years after the last crisis unemployment did not fall below the high mark of the previous crisis year, 1921. Only when the rearmament drive began did unemployment start to decline to what may be regarded as the "normal" post-war 1914–18 level, which is two or three times as high as the pre-war 1914–18 level. During the present war unemployment has also declined, but not as rapidly as during the first year of the war-period 1914–18.

But unemployment was not only high generally throughout the country. In some parts of Britain—the so-called distressed areas—unemployment, during all the years after the crisis of 1921, remained on a level which often surpassed the crisis peak for the country as a whole. In some parts of the country—industrially active during the last war, and almost dead during the succeeding years of peace—unemployment was rarely below 25 per cent, and sometimes reached 50 per cent and more. In the distressed areas unemployment was not merely a menace rendering existence harassingly uncertain; unemployment was a certainty, the normal thing. In these parts of the country living conditions deteriorated very rapidly. Communities became so impoverished that they were unable to continue many services regarded nowadays as basically necessary: schools closed down because children lacked clothes and shoes and could not attend, and there were no funds for teachers' salaries; many small tradesmen became bankrupt because people could no longer buy enough to keep their shops going. Many a small place became completely derelict, and some towns of not inconsiderable size at least partly so.

Furthermore, with the labour market glutted because of relatively low production and the increasing productivity per hour, the employers tended to discriminate against the older age groups, and thus came into existence a core of some hundreds of thousands of men who for many months, and even for years, could not find employment because they lived in derelict areas or because of their age.*

PERCENTAGE OF UNEMPLOYED WHO WERE UNEMPLOYED FOR A YEAR OR MORE

Date	Percentage
December 1932	21·1
December 1933	25·4
December 1934	24·2
December 1935	26·5
December 1936	25·1
December 1937	21·3
December 1938	19·3
August 1939	25·8

These figures show the terrible extent of unemployment. One-fifth to one-quarter of all unemployed were workless for a year or more. Many of them, in fact, the majority, were unemployed for longer than two years:*

PERCENTAGE OF LONG-TERM UNEMPLOYED IN AUGUST 1939

Unemployed for at least 1 but less than 2 years	34·6
Unemployed for at least 2 but less than 3 years	19·3
Unemployed for at least 3 but less than 4 years	16·4
Unemployed for at least 4 but less than 5 years	7·6
Unemployed for 5 or more years	22·1

* Cf. *The Ministry of Labour Gazette*, February 1940.

Thus, more than one-fifth of all the long-term unemployed had had no work for five years or more! They had really lost their quality of workers—they had become "pensioners" for life, living on a pittance; they had lost all the skill they once possessed; they had lost all hope of working again; most of them were not living but vegetating, victims of capitalism in decay.

*   *   *

Another factor which has a detrimental influence on the life of the workers is the high rate of accidents. It is about one hundred years since the first safety and sanitary regulations were framed by the Government affecting conditions of the workers in their employment. Yet it is doubtful whether the rate of accidents has declined. A whole art of accident prevention has been developed; many safety devices of great ingenuity have been perfected; but the intensity of labour and the consequent fatigue of the worker have increased to such a degree that the benefit which science and invention have achieved has been undone by the evils which cut-throat competition and intensive exploitation have brought about. Unfortunately, there are no reliable accident statistics going back for any length of time. Only in the mining industry have we statistics which can give us a rough idea of the development of the rate of fatal accidents.*

DEATH RATE IN COAL-MINING ACCIDENTS

Years	Rate per 1,000 Employed
1893–1902	1·39
1903–12	1·33
1913–22	1·15
1923–32	1·05
1933–41	1·12

The death rate has declined slightly according to these figures. But they are misleading, for they refer to one thousand employed and do not take into account the length of the working day. Assuming the working day in the first period under review to be about eight and a half hours, and during the last period under review somewhat less than eight hours, and assuming that the number of shifts per annum worked was about the same, we find that each thousand miners in the most recent period were

* Cf. Annual Reports of the Secretary for Mines and Hansard, January 21, 1942.

exposed to the risk of accidents for 7–9 per cent fewer hours than in the first period under review. Now the fatal accident rate has declined during the whole time under review by about 20 per cent. This means that the accident rate per hour of exposure has declined over fifty years by only little more than 10 per cent, while over the last twenty-five years it has, in fact, increased! Since the number of shifts worked annually has, actually, been smaller between 1923 and 1941 than between 1893 and 1912 it should not be surprising if the accident rate per hour of work has actually increased during the last fifty years.

It is improbable that the non-fatal accident rate has improved during a period in which the fatal accident rate has either declined very little or may even have increased. If the employers are inclined at all to avoid accidents—that is, to sacrifice a small part of their profits to prevent them—it is with the fatal accident that they are concerned, for, as non-fatal accidents are so numerous and of daily occurence, they do not fear any serious reaction of the workers against them. While it is significant that no reliable non-fatal accident statistics are published—and the motive is easily comprehensible—we can assume from the few data available that during the twentieth century their rate has increased rather than declined. While working conditions in many respects have been improved (better lighting, ventilation, etc.) the increased pace at which the worker has to labour has more than cancelled out these improvements. In fact, a number of such improvements have been made for the express purpose of increasing the intensity of work. On the whole, therefore, working conditions to-day are more detrimental to the health of the worker than they were at the beginning of the century. Just as one hundred years ago Engels could quote a medical authority as saying that those workers who stayed away from the factories for some time (even if they spent this time in drinking or sleeping off the effects of too much alcohol) had a longer expectation of life than those who worked regularly, because of the terrible conditions in the factories, so can we say to-day that most of the improvements in working conditions have been made to further the intensification of labour, and that the speed-up resulting from these improvements, as well as the general speed-up, have tended to worsen health conditions.

This estimate of the situation has recently found support in a most valuable study on "Factory Inspection: A Thirty-Five Years Retrospect," by Sir Duncan Wilson.* Comparing industrial accidents in the beginning of this century and at the end of the thirties, he comes to the conclusion:

"But there is one aspect of industry in which we have progressed little if at all—and that is accident incidence. . . . The accident risk seems to have been little affected by all the attention and skill that has been devoted to its study."

Since Sir Duncan Wilson arrives at this conclusion without taking into account the shortening of the working day which has taken place during the last forty years, it is obvious that his estimate of the situation would have been even more pessimistic if he had studied accident incidence not only per employed worker but also per hour worked, that is, per hour of exposure to industrial accidents.

*   *   *

We have frequently referred in the foregoing pages to the increased intensity of work. That this has increased rapidly is a fact recognized by everybody. But nobody knows by how much it has been increased. Nobody has even been able to form an estimate. The only computation which can be made is that of the increase in general productivity, that is, the increase of production per worker and per hour. This increase, however, is not due solely to the increased intensity of labour per worker, but partly also to technical improvements which do not necessarily require a corresponding increase in the effort put forth by the worker.

EMPLOYMENT, PRODUCTION AND PRODUCTIVITY, 1880 TO 1939†

(*1913 = 100*)

Trade Cycle	Employment	Production	Productivity
1880–86	73	57	79
1887–95	80	65	81
1895–1903	87	75	85
1904–08	91	83	91
1909–14	97	91	93
1924–32	95	90	95
1933–39	101	108	106

* Read before the Royal Statistical Society on May 20, 1941.

† Figures for individual years, see Appendix to Chapter III, 1900 to the Present Day.

If we look first at the figures of employment we find that up to the first world war there was a steady rise, but that from the years immediately preceding the first world war until the middle of the thirties, there was little change in the labour force actually employed. The reason for this is not a sudden stoppage in the flow of new workers into the labour market; it is not a sudden increase in deaths of older workers as compared with the inflow of younger workers; it is not a sudden prosperity of the working class which induced many to quit the labour market sooner than is usual because they could live on their savings; the real cause is the rapid rise in unemployment in the years following the first world war; and the root cause for the considerable increase in unemployment is the decay of British capitalism.

Almost the same movement took place as far as production is concerned. Here, too, we can observe a sudden cessation of growth in the years following the first world war.

Before we study the figures of productivity it should be mentioned, however, that the above table shows only the productivity per worker. Though our data as to the development of the number of hours worked per day are too scanty to take into account changes in the length of the working day if we calculate year-to-year indices, it is possible to take into account roughly the shortening of the working day if we calculate trade cycle averages. Unfortunately, we have no data showing variations in short-time work, so that we have to leave this factor out of account. We repeat in the following table the statistics of productivity per worker and add estimates of the productivity per worker per hour.

THE PRODUCTIVITY PER WORKER

($1913 = 100$)

Trade Cycles	Productivity per Worker	Productivity per Worker and per Hour
1880–86	79	71
1887–95	81	75
1895–1903	85	80
1904–08	91	87
1909–14	93	93
1924–32	95	105
1933–39	106	119

Productivity per worker per hour has increased during the last sixty years by about 70 per cent at least; I say "at least" because short-time, which has not been taken into account, was more widespread in the nineteen-thirties than in the eighties of the last century. The increase has been fairly equally spread over the years preceding and those following the last world war; if one were able to take into account the spread of short-time one would probably find a small acceleration in post-war years.

But it is of more importance that, if one were able to construct a special index of the increased intensity of work—that is of increased productivity caused, not by improved machinery, but by more intense, more strenuous work by the individual worker— one would undoubtedly find a considerable acceleration in post-war years. This acceleration is one of the chief causes of the poor health, and especially of the nervous diseases, affecting so many industrial workers, and of the high level of industrial accidents.

*   *   *

When the worker returns in the evening, dead tired, with a wage often not sufficient to keep himself and his family fit, he often comes to a home that is noisy, overcrowded and insanitary. Much has been made of the post-war building programme and the improvements it has brought about. But if we look at the census figures, we find that very little change has indeed taken place. The following table gives the "incidence of sub-standard housing conditions," that is, the percentage of persons living more than two per room, for English county boroughs as well as for the country as a whole:*

INCIDENCE OF SUB-STANDARD HOUSING CONDITIONS
(*1901 to 1931*)

Years	County Boroughs	Country as a Whole
1901	7·8	8·2
1911	7·7	7·8
1921	9·4	8·5
1931	7·2	6·2

* Cf. P. D'Arcy Hart and G. Payling Wright, *Tuberculosis and Social Conditions in England*, London, 1939, pp. 57, 109.

There was an extremely small improvement in the years preceding the last war; the war years brought, of course, a considerable deterioration; post-war development drove the housing standard in the county borough only little above the pre-war level, while for the country as a whole conditions improved somewhat more. To-day, conditions are deteriorating again.

If one remembers the investigation of Dr. M'Gonigle, and then realizes that the small pre-war improvement has been secured, in some instances, at the cost of a rapid deterioration in food conditions, one hardly dares to praise the post-war housing policy, and the housing conditions of the workers.

*   *   *

One characteristic feature in the development of labour conditions in the period under review should receive some special attention. We recall that during the first period of industrial capitalism exploitation consisted to a large extent in the creation of absolute surplus value—more hours of work per day, employment of children on a grand scale, lowering of real wages, etc. During the second period, it was chiefly relative surplus value that was created; the working day was shortened, the percentage of skilled workers and the degree of skill increased, real wages increased, and work was enormously intensified. During the third period, especially during its last stage, finance capital and monopoly try to combine both methods. This can best be observed in Germany, where, according to official statements since the Fascist Government came to power, child labour is again on the increase, the working day has been lengthened, and labour is diluted, while nevertheless the intensity of work increases.*

This is happening in Britain too. Real wages have declined since the turn of the century. The working day in the mines before the present war had already become longer than in the years following the last war. Dilution of labour continued in all industries. The employment of women has been spreading. Before the war it was not unusual to hear of husbands being un-

---

* Cf. Jürgen Kuczynski, *The Condition of the Workers in Great Britain, Germany and the Soviet Union, 1932–38.*

employed while wives endeavoured to earn a few shillings at some employment.*

These are the beginnings of barbarism: intensive exploitation through the creation of absolute and relative surplus value by employing the primitive methods of one hundred years ago and the more recently developed methods of extraction. Capitalism in decay begins again to use the primitive means of exploitation in addition to its more "refined" methods. If capitalism continues in power one may expect a further lengthening of the working day, and child labour may be introduced either surreptitiously or officially. The quicker consumption of man-power will not bother the ruling class because of the large industrial reserve army composed of many hundred thousands of unemployed.

When we say that the most reactionary elements of the ruling class are in power, we refer, as far as labour conditions are concerned, to that group which does not object to reverting to the primitive methods of industrial capitalism in order to find additional means of squeezing more profits out of the people.

* * *

Surveying the period now under review, the years from the turn of the century to the present world war, we find that the British workers have had to endure:

> One minor war (South African War).
> Two world wars (1914–18 and 1939–).
> One severe crisis (1908).
> Two terrible world crises (1921–22 and 1929–32).
> Several minor recessions.
> One period of serious inflationary policy (1915–20).

The years of world war meant death and disablement to many hundreds of thousands of British workers. The economic losses of the working class, the burdens imposed upon them, the savings of which they were robbed, the diversion of their labour to production of the means of destruction instead of useful goods—all this defies adequate description. How can one multiply by the hundred thousand the feelings of a mother who sees her children going hungry day after day, the feelings of a wife who

* The same could be observed one hundred years ago. Cf. p. 45 of this book.

loses her husband, or receives him back a cripple! The statistician and economist frankly admits himself to be unequal to this task, while knowing, as a politician, that the realization even of one-millionth of what such wars mean to them must rouse the masses of the people to end the conditions which produce these wars.

While unable to express the suffering and grief which a world crisis brings about, the statistician is able to measure roughly its economic consequences. And the result of such measurement, for instance, is that the 1929–32 crisis cost the working class economically about as much as the world war, if not more.

It is obvious that a period of capitalism which includes so many severe crises and two world wars must have meant a very considerable deterioration of labour and living conditions as compared with the previous period. And since the previous period (comprising the second half of the nineteenth century) brought a deterioration of conditions as compared with the first period (comprising the first seventy-five years of industrial capitalism), we can now say that, in spite of the enormous technical progress, in spite of the phenomenal increase in the production of commodities, in spite of the vast wealth created, the working class has experienced a constant worsening of conditions, not in all respects, not always in the same respect, not for all its sections always, but taking all aspects of labour and living conditions together.

Some people will say that the workers and their families are eating more and better to-day than fifty or a hundred years ago. Right! But the workers need more food because they have to work more intensely, and in fact the intensity of work has increased more than the quantity and quality of food they consume. Some people will say that the workers have more leisure to-day than fifty or a hundred years ago. Right! But the workers come home from work so exhausted that without increased leisure they would not be able to work at the pace required to-day in industry. Some will say that the introduction of social legislation has brought more security to the workers. Right! But increased and long-time unemployment have brought much more insecurity into the worker's life than the pittance paid through unemployment insurance can compensate. Old age sets in much earlier to-day than fifty years ago because the older worker is often sacked for life and the meagre unemployment benefit or old age pension cannot make up for the working years a wage earner still had before him half a century ago at the age of fifty. Some people will say that the death rate has declined and that dangerous epidemics have been prevented and that health conditions in general have improved. True, the death rate has declined and dangerous epidemics have disappeared. But that does not mean that the worker has become healthier or that he has more chance of enjoying his prolonged life.

Whenever we are able to point to improvements we are at the same time, unfortunately, obliged to point to deteriorations which over-compensate the improvements in the condition of the working class during the last fifty or hundred years.

Industrial capitalism has laid the technical foundations for a better life for mankind—but the society built on these foundations is all wrong. The house of national economy has rooms for all the people, but the majority to-day are congested in a few, and are fed just enough to keep them alive, enough to enable them to continue building better and bigger rooms for the tiny minority which forms the ruling class. Only a complete reconstruction can provide the masses with the standard of comfort which technical progress, the means of production and the skill of the people could enable them to have.

*   *   *

While absolute labour conditions deteriorated considerably, and while the wealth of the country increased and the rich profited thereby, it is obvious that relative conditions must also have deteriorated.

RELATIVE WAGES, 1895 TO 1932

(1900 = 100)

Cycles	Industrial per capita production	Real Wages	Relative Wages	Share of Capital*
1859–68	51	63	124	81
1895–1903	105	99	94	106
1904–08	104	95	91	110
1909–14	106	93	88	114
1924–32	119	91	76	132

* See text and footnote on p. 82 of this book.

Thus, the relative position of the worker has worsened from cycle to cycle, and during the last full trade cycle, 1924–32, it was lower by about 40 per cent than during the sixties of the last century. At the same time the share of the capitalists* has increased during the same period by over 60 per cent.

The abyss between the two nations, between the poor and the rich, between the millions and the few, between the people and its ruling class, has widened enormously. Capital has made gigantic gains, and labour's position in capitalist society has become worse than one would have thought possible in the sixties of the previous century when Karl Marx published *Capital* and when the First International—whose leadership included the prominent trade union leaders of Britain—hoped for a speedy delivery of the people from the evils of capitalism.

*   *   *

The new period in the history of industrial capitalism can also be studied in its reflection in the history of the British labour movement, which likewise entered upon its third phase at about this time. The beginnings of this new period in the history of the labour movement under industrial capitalism can be traced back to the eighties of the last century.

While the topic of piece-work, when introduced by a delegate at the 1876 Trade Union Congress, was still regarded as one not to be mentioned by a respectable trade unionist, and as being too "anarchistic" and close to the sordidness of every-day life, and while still, in the early eighties, as the Webbs rightly observe,† "all observers were agreed that the Trade Unions of Great Britain would furnish an impenetrable barrier against Socialistic projects," all this changed in the second half of the eighties, and by 1893 (September 11) we find *The Times* regretfully and alarmedly noting that a new spirit dominated the Trade Union Congress.

How did this change come about? Some say that the organization of the Social Democratic Federation, in the beginning of the eighties, helped to permeate the trade unions with a new spirit. Great influence was often attributed to the lecturing tours

* See text and footnote on p. 82 of this book.   † L.c. p. 374.

by men like William Morris and H. M. Hyndman, who not only reminded the workers how badly off they were but also explained the causes for this and showed how they could change society. But new ideologies alone—or, rather, old ideologies newly presented in better (or worse) form—do not change the labour movement. Something else is needed to make the workers ready to listen and to act. What were the new material facts?

Let us look at economic conditions during the eighties and early nineties:

1880	Increasing trade activity.
1881	Increasing trade activity.
1882	Increasing trade activity.
1883	Recession.
1884	Crisis.
1885	Crisis.
1886	Depression.
1887	Increasing trade activity.
1888	Increasing trade activity.
1889	Increasing trade activity.
1890	Increasing trade activity.
1891	Recession.
1892	Crisis.
1893	Crisis.

Between 1883–93 we note four years of increasing trade activity and seven years of recession, crisis or depression. Unemployment increased considerably. The town of Jarrow, so ill-famed after the last war and during the 1930's for its unemployment conditions, is frequently mentioned when the plight of the unemployed is described. Robert Knight, in the Boiler-makers' Annual Report for 1886,* writes:

"In every shipbuilding port there are to be seen thousands of idle men vainly seeking for an honest day's work. The privation that has been endured by them, their wives and children, is terrible to contemplate. Sickness has been very prevalent, whilst the hundreds of pinched and hungry faces have told a tale of suffering and privation which no optimism could minimize or conceal."

General conditions, misery, hunger and unemployment for year after year, made the workers ready to hear the new message. But not only the workers in general; the skilled trades suffered

* Quoted by the Webbs, l.c. p. 378.

equally, if not more so. So exclusive and aristocratic an organization as the Union of Flint Glass Makers permitted its secretary to write: "To our minds it is very hard for employers to attempt to force men into systems by which they cannot earn an honourable living."*

During the former period, we have seen the trade unions often deprecating strikes and acting chiefly as benevolent institutions for the benefit (unemployment, burial, emigration, old age, etc.) of their members; in the eighties, year after year of poor trade conditions depleted the funds of the strongest skilled workers' union; benefits were reduced while contributions were increased and many members, old trade unionists, highly skilled men, aristocrats of labour, were left stranded. The old trade union idea was not able to weather such a storm. It proved weak and insufficient in the face of the cruel realities of approaching imperialism, of the beginnings of capitalism in decay and turmoil. The old trade unions were condemned by the brutal economic facts of life, and by the workers who found them inadequate.

We may therefore assert that, during the first period of the British labour movement under industrial capitalism, politics was the guiding star of all workers' organizations, including the numerous short-lived unions. During the second period the British working class learned the fundamental principles of organization. And now, in this third period, they were learning how to build up a labour movement which should be both strongly organized and also permeated with political ideas to be realized through organized action.

In the course of a few years, the new leaders of labour, strongly influenced by socialist ideas, gained a decisive influence in the labour movement, especially the trade unions. Political parties, the Social Democratic Federation, the Socialist League, the Scottish Labour Party, the Labour Party and the Independent Labour Party, sprang up and permeated the trade unions, gaining a large following among their members.

At the same time, trade union organization began among the unskilled workers. The strike of the dockers in 1889, led by Ben Tillett, Tom Mann and John Burns; the success of the new Gas Workers' and General Labourers' Union, established

* *Flint Glass Makers' Magazine*, November 1884.

in 1889 and formed with the help of Burns, Mann and Tillett; the historic strike of the match-girls; the unemployed movements leading up to the famous demonstration on Sunday, November 13, 1887, in Trafalgar Square; all this spread the new ideas and caused them deeply to penetrate the consciousness of the British proletariat.

Quite rightly, the Webbs say,* "The student of the volumes of *Justice* between 1884 and 1889 will be struck by the unconscious resemblance of many of the ideas and much of the phraseology of its contributors, to those of the *Poor Man's Guardian* and the *Pioneer* of 1834." But they omit to mention that the men who expressed those similar ideas had accumulated in their minds the experiences of the working class in the intervening fifty years and that they spoke, not for a loosely organized body of workers, but for well-disciplined mass organizations.

Unfortunately, the strike records of the British labour movement have been very badly kept and we have comprehensive data at our disposal only since 1888. But even so, a survey since then is very instructive. But before we look at the following table it is necessary to say a few words about the significance of strikes as an expression of working-class activity. Strikes are not only the most important sign of militancy in the labour movement, they are also the only statistical measure of the intensity of pressure and resistance which the workers show against the employers. For this reason, an analysis of the strike activity of the workers in a study like the present takes a prominent place in the pages devoted to a brief sketch of some important phases of the labour movement. (The reader must remember that the greatest revolutionary in this century, Lenin, based a considerable part of his analysis of the 1905 revolution on a detailed study of the strike movement.) At the same time it is necessary to remember that strikes are not the only expression of militancy, of a purposeful and well-guided labour movement. I do not know of any case in which the labour movement was militant and progressive while at the same time strike activity was low, but it is equally true to say that the militancy of the labour movement cannot and does not find exclusive expression in strike activities.

* L.c. p. 409.

ECONOMIC CONDITIONS AND STRIKE ACTIVITIES, 1888 TO 1914

Year	Economic Conditions	Unemployment	Days of Strike Millions*	Percentage of Unsuccessfully striking Workers
1888	Improving	Declining	—†	24·0‡
1889	Improving	Declining	—§	12·0
1890	Improving	Declining	7·3	25·9
1891	Recession	Increasing	6·8	34·8
1892	Crisis	High	17·4	19·9
1893	Crisis	High	31·2	12·1
1894	Improving	Declining	9·3	42·1
1895	Improving	Declining	5·5	27·9
1896	Improving	Declining	3·7	33·4
1897	Improving	Slight Incr.	10·3	40·7
1898	Improving	Declining	15·3	60·1
1899	Improving	Declining	2·5	43·7
1900	Recession	Increasing	3·2	27·5
1901	Crisis	Increasing	4·1	34·7
1902	Crisis	Increasing	3·5	31·8
1903	Depression	High	2·3	48·1
1904	Depression	High	1·5	41·7
1905	Improving	Declining	2·5	34·0
1906	Improving	Declining	3·0	24·5
1907	Improving	Slight Incr.	2·2	27·3
1908	Crisis	High	10·8	25·7
1909	Depression	High	2·8	22·3
1910	Improving	Declining	9·9	13·8
1911	Improving	Declining	10·3	9·3
1912	Improving	Slight Incr.	40·9	14·4
1913	Improving	Declining	9·8	18·8
1914	Recession War	Increasing	9·9	14·9

This table demonstrates the marked virility of the labour movement in the early nineties, and even, one can say, up to the 1914–18 war. The years of crisis and high unemployment in the nineties did not damp the labour movement, nor, in particular, did it deter the trade unions from striking. On the contrary, strike activity increased in 1892 and 1893; it was higher during the crisis years 1901 and 1902 than during the two preceding years; it increased rapidly during the crisis year 1908 and remained on a high level during the years 1910–14,

* Computed by multiplying the number of days struck and the number of men taking part in the strike.
† The number of workers striking was 119,000.
‡ The 1888 figure refers to the percentage of strikes which were unsuccessful, not to the percentage of workers which struck unsuccessfully.
§ The number of workers striking in 1889 and 1890 was 360,000 and 393,000.

following upon the depression of 1909. Moreover, the percentage of unsuccessful strikes was relatively very low during the crisis years 1892 and 1893; it was lower during the crisis years 1900 to 1902 than during the preceding years of increasing trade activity; and it remained on a low level during the crisis and the following years of increasing trade activity from 1908–14.

Labour's record during the twenty-six years under review is a good one. Many wage cuts planned by the employers were prevented through strike action; many wage increases and reductions in the working day were secured; and there is no doubt that had the labour movement, especially the trade unions, during this period, not been as active as they proved to be, the full impact of the new position of British capitalism would have been felt more acutely by the workers than was the case.

Then came the war and the collapse of the official labour movement. The shop steward movement in the later stages of the war came to the rescue of labour and, as the following table shows, there developed a new and active drive for better conditions.

ECONOMIC CONDITIONS AND STRIKE ACTIVITIES, 1914 TO 1922

Year	Economic Conditions	Unemployment	Days of Strike Millions	Percentage of Unsuccessfully Striking Workers
1914	Recession, War	Increasing	9·9	14·9
1915	War	Declining	3·0	14·1
1916	War	Very Low	2·4	29·8
1917	War	Very Low	5·6	13·3
1918	War	Very Low	5·9	22·1
1919	Improving	Increasing	35·0	23·9
1920	Improving	Stable	26·6	10·6
1921	Crisis	Very High	85·9	5·6
1922	Depression	Very High	19·9	12·5

During the war, we note that there was first a rapid decline in strike activity, the low point being reached in 1916, a year also when the employers were relatively most successful in defeating strikes and ending them without having to compromise. In 1917, the situation changed, strike activity increased up to 1919, had a slight relapse in 1920, and reached new heights during the crisis year, 1921, during which year also the employers were least successful in defeating strikes, although the workers usually had to be satisfied with compromise settlements. In 1922 strike activity fell rapidly.

Yet these figures do not tell the whole story. We must note that in 1920 the coal miners were responsible for 16·0 out of 26·6 million strike days, and these same miners in 1921 accounted for 72·0 out of 85·9 million days, while in 1919 there was a national railway strike accounting for 3·9 million days, a national strike of the cotton operatives accounting for 7·5 million days, and a miners' strike in Yorkshire accounting for 3·8 million days. We can then realize that the backbone of strike activity had really been broken by 1920, and that in 1920 and 1921 aggressive labour action was being prosecuted chiefly by one large union which seemed to have but small influence on the labour movement as a whole; the relatively high figure of 1922 is accounted for to the extent of two-thirds by the action of the engineers who struck for 13·7 men-days out of 19·9.

The vigorous pre-war years did not return. The labour leadership had been broken in by the ruling class during the war, and no new leadership was ready to take over and carry on to fresh and bigger struggles. The new militancy, which began in the latter years of the war, was soon suppressed, at least to some extent.

ECONOMIC CONDITIONS AND STRIKE ACTIVITIES, 1922 TO 1940

Year	Economic Conditions	Unemployment	Days of Strike Millions	Percentage of Unsuccessfully Striking Workers
1922	Depression	Declining	19·9	12·5
1923	Improving	Declining	10·7	23·1
1924	Improving	Declining	8·4	18·0
1925	Recession	Increasing	8·0	14·4
1926	Depression	Increasing	162·2	35·6
1927	Improving	Declining	1·2	30·6
1928	Recession	Increasing	1·4	39·3
1929	Improving	Declining	8·3	6·9
1930	Crisis	Very High	4·4	77·8
1931	Crisis	Very High	7·0	15·6
1932	Depression	Very High	6·5	47·3
1933	Improving	Very High	1·1	42·0
1934	Improving	Declining	1·0	32·7
1935	Improving	Declining	2·0	27·2
1936	Improving	Declining	1·8	49·6
1937	Improving	Declining	3·4	63·6
1938	Recession	Increasing	1·3	53·6
1939	Improving, War	Declining	1·4	51·2
1940	War	Declining	0·9	—

The picture which these figures reveal is a sorry one. The

year of the General Strike was an isolated one. The workers had not been trained to mass action. The years preceding the General Strike were years of declining strike activity. In 1923 no single strike involving one hundred thousand workers or more took place; in 1924 we have two strikes just reaching that figure: a short one of the dockers and a longer one of the building trade workers. In 1925, again we try in vain to find a strike of one hundred thousand or more workers. And then follows the year of catastrophe and treachery: the year of the General Strike. Full of enthusiasm, angered by the provocative economic policy of the Government, but unprepared and led by partly unwilling, and politically weak leaders (Thomas, MacDonald, etc.), the labour movement entered upon that gigantic venture to be beaten in nine days in spite of a magnificent response by the whole of the rank and file, by default of their own leadership. Of the 162·2 million strike days, only 15·0 are accounted for by the larger labour movement taking part in the General Strike, while the coal miners account for 145·2 million days; only one million strike days immediately precede or follow the General Strike. In the following years the labour movement seemed to have broken down completely. In 1929 there first appeared to be a revival, but the succeeding crisis, instead of bringing to the forefront the most militant labour leaders and stimulating real activity on the part of the trade unions*—as was the case in so many former years of economic crisis—resulted only in a renewed decline of strike activity. After the crisis something unprecedented occurred: for seven whole years there was not a single strike involving at least one hundred thousand or more workers. It looked as though the British workers had forgotten how to strike, and that the labour movement had been dealt a death-blow. The history of the last two years, however, shows that a new leadership is emerging, basing itself to a large extent on the experience which the most advanced workers in

---

* Trade union membership—which in 1900 had reached the two million mark and which, during the active years from 1910 to 1914 rose from 2·6 to 4·1 millions, and then during the war and after the active years up to 1920 reached a record figure of 8·3 millions—shrank rapidly after the break in labour activity in 1920; it fell to 5·5 millions in 1925 and since 1927 has remained below or just above the five million mark. Only in the last two years it has begun to rise again appreciably.

the Labour Party and the trade unions, in the Minority Movement and the unemployed workers' organizations, and in the Communist Party, had gained in their attempts to inspire labour with a spirit of militancy, the spirit necessary for a fight for better working and living conditions. Old barriers are breaking down. A new era in the history of British labour is beginning.*

To-day all groups and parties of the labour movement are joined in one common goal: to beat the common enemy of international labour, of all the freedom-loving peoples: German Fascism.

APPENDIX TO CHAPTER III

1900 TO THE PRESENT DAY

I. TABLES

1. AN INDEX OF UNPRODUCTIVITY, 1880 TO 1939

(1880 = 100)

Year	Inroads in Labour Force through Unemployment (Full Labour Force equals 100)	Inroads in Labour Force through Unemployment and Over-Employment of Unproductive Forces	Percentage of National Income spent on Armaments	Index of Unproductivity
1880	94·5	94	2·7	100
1881	96·5	96	2·3	98
1882	97·7	97	2·3	97
1883	97·4	97	2·6	98
1884	91·9	91	2·4	103
1885	90·7	90	2·7	105
1886	89·8	89	3·4	107
1887	92·4	91	2·7	104
1888	95·1	94	2·4	101
1889	97·9	96	2·2	98
1890	97·9	96	2·4	98
1891	96·5	94	2·4	100
1892	93·7	91	2·4	103
1893	92·5	90	2·4	105
1894	93·1	90	2·4	104
1895	94·2	91	2·6	103
1896	96·7	94	2·7	101
1897	96·7	94	2·6	101
1898	97·2	94	2·7	101
1899	98·0	94	4·0	102

* A short and excellent outline of the history of the trade union movement since 1914 is given in Allen Hutt's book, *British Trade Unionism*, Chapters 6 to 10.

1. AN INDEX OF UNPRODUCTIVITY, 1880 TO 1939—*continued*

1800 = 100

Year	Inroads in Labour Force through Unemployment (Full Labour Force equals 100)	Inroads in Labour Force through Unemployment and Over-Employment of Unproductive Forces	Percentage of National Income spent on Armaments	Index of Unproductivity
1900	97·5	93	6·8	106
1901	96·7	92	7·3	107
1902	96·0	91	6·4	107
1903	95·3	90	4·5	106
1904	94·0	90	4·3	107
1905	95·0	90	3·8	106
1906	96·4	91	3·3	105
1907	96·3	90	3·1	105
1908	92·2	86	3·2	110
1909	92·3	86	3·4	111
1910	95·3	88	3·4	108
1911	97·0	89	3·4	106
1912	96·8	89	3·3	107
1913	97·9	90	3·5	106
1914	96·7	88	19·4	129
1915	98·9	90	50·0	203
1916	99·6	91	56·3	231
1917	99·3	91	53·4	217
1918	99·2	91	40·0	169
1919	97·6	89	11·5	116
1920	97·6	88	4·5	109
1921	83·4	75	4·2	128
1922	85·9	77	2·8	122
1923	88·4	80	2·5	119
1924	89·8	81	2·6	117
1925	89·0	80	2·5	118
1926	87·7	78	2·6	120
1927	90·4	81	2·5	117
1928	89·3	80	2·4	118
1929	89·7	80	2·4	118
1930	84·2	75	2·4	126
1931	78·9	70	2·5	135
1932	78·1	69	2·4	136
1933	80·2	71	2·5	133
1934	83·4	74	2·4	128
1935	84·7	75	2·7	127
1936	87·1	76	3·5	125
1937	89·4	78	4·5	123
1938	87·5	77	7·0	129
1939	88·7	77	19·0	147

2. WAGE RATES IN INDIVIDUAL INDUSTRIES, 1900–1940

(1900 = 100)

End of Year	Building	Coal Mining	Engineering	Textiles	Agriculture
1900	100	100	100	100	100
1901	100	94	100	100	100
1902	100	88	100	100	101
1903	100	85	100	100	102
1904	100	82	100	100	102
1905	100	81	100	103	103
1906	100	83	101	106	103
1907	100	96	102	109	103
1908	100	93	102	109	104
1909	100	89	102	107	104
1910	100	90	102	107	105
1911	101	89	104	107	106
1912	102	94	105	111	107
1913	105	100	106	112	111
1914†	108	99	107	112	114
1915*	110	112	122§	120	128‖
1916*	120	127	134§	127	—
1917*	138	134	154	142	—
1918*	184	184	206	178	216¶
1919*	220	220	242	224	258**
1920‡	288	256	288	282	290**
1921	262	192††	265	225	234
1922	205	130	175	198	181
1923	199	139	172	198	181
1924	211	143	179	198	181
1925	212	143	179	197	199
1926	213	142	179	197	201
1927	214	130	179	196	201
1928	209	124	180	195	200
1929	208	123	180	187	200
1930	205	122	181	183	199
1931	201	120	181	178	196
1932	194	120	175	169	195
1933	188	120	175	169	193
1934	189	120	176	169	194
1935	193	120	181	167	200
1936	202	130	187	174	202
1937	211	139	196	181	212
1938	217	139	201	181	220
1939*	219	139	201	181	221
1940‡‡	239	166	227	215	309

    * July figures for 1914 to 1920, and for 1939.
    † The December figures are: Building, 108; Coal mining, 98; Engineering, 107; Textiles, 112; and Agriculture, 115.
    ‡ The December figures are: Building, 307; Coal mining, 282 (earnings fourth quarter); Engineering, 288; Textiles, 303; Agriculture, 297.
    § December figures.   ‖ April.   ¶ August.
  ** May.   †† Earnings fourth quarter.   ‡‡ Estimate for October.

3. WAGES IN THE UNITED KINGDOM

(1900 = 100)

Year End of	Gross Money Wages*	Net Money Wages†	Net Real Wages per Full-Time Week‡	Net Real Wages per Unemployed and Employed Worker	Cost of Living
1900	100	100	100	100	100
1901	99	98	107	106	93
1902	98	96	98	97	100
1903	97	95	97	95	101
1904	97	93	96	93	101
1905	97	95	96	94	101
1906	99	98	98	97	101
1907	102	101	99	97	104
1908	102	96	97	92	105
1909	100	95	96	90	105
1910	101	98	95	93	106
1911	101	101	95	94	107
1912	104	101	93	92	110
1913	107	106	95	95	111
1914§	108	105	97	96	110
1915‖	116	116	83	84	138
1916‖	127	128	78	80	160
1917‖	149	149	74	75	198
1918‖	192	192	84	85	226
1919‖	230	227	98	98	231
1920¶	281	277	100	100	277
1921	227	197	100	92	215
1922	187	165	90	84	197
1923	184	165	90	85	195
1924	190	172	91	87	198
1925	191	172	94	89	194
1925	192	172	93	88	196
1927	188	171	97	92	185
1928	186	168	96	91	184
1929	185	167	96	91	183
1930	184	161	103	95	170
1931	179	148	104	91	162
1932	177	145	106	93	157
1933	176	147	105	94	157
1934	177	152	105	96	158
1935	178	154	103	95	162
1936	183	163	105	98	166
1937	191	173	104	98	176
1938	193	172	107	100	172
1939	197	178	98	94	190
1940	217	—	—	—	214

For footnotes see p. 132.

4. PRODUCTION AND PRODUCTIVITY, 1880 TO 1939

(1913 = 100)

Year	Employment	Production	Productivity
1880	70	55	78
1881	73	55	76
1882	74	59	79
1883	75	61	80
1884	72	59	82
1885	72	57	80
1886	72	56	78
1887	75	58	78
1888	77	63	81
1889	81	67	83
1890	81	67	82
1891	81	67	82
1892	80	63	80
1893	79	62	78
1894	81	66	82
1895	82	68	83
1896	85	72	84
1897	86	72	84
1898	87	75	85
1899	89	78	88
1900	89	78	87
1901	89	76	85
1902	90	78	87
1903	90	78	86
1904	89	77	86
1905	91	82	91
1906	93	86	92
1907	94	87	93
1908	90	82	91
1909	91	83	91
1910	95	87	91
1911	98	89	92
1912	98	91	93
1913	100	100	100
1914	100	93	93

Footnotes to p. 131.

* Without taking into account wage losses and gains through short-time, unemployment, taxes, social insurance contributions, social insurance benefits, etc.

† Taking into account wage losses through unemployment and social insurance contributions (since 1912) and wage gains through unemployment insurance benefits (since 1921).

‡ Taking into account social insurance contributions.

§ The corresponding figures for December are gross money wages 108 and cost of living 110.

‖ July figures for 1914 to 1920.

¶ The corresponding figures for December are: gross money wages 292 and cost of living 294.

4. PRODUCTION AND PRODUCTIVITY, 1880 TO 1939—*continued*

($1931 = 100$)

Year	Employment	Production	Productivity
1920	102	91	89
1921	88	62	70
1922	91	77	84
1923	94	83	88
1924	96	88	92
1925	96	87	91
1926	95	(77)*	—
1927	99	94	96
1928	98	93	95
1929	99	99	100
1930	94	91	97
1931	89	83	93
1932	88	82	93
1933	91	87	95
1934	95	96	102
1935	98	103	106
1936	102	113	111
1937	108	121	113
1938	107	113	106
1939†	109	120	110

II. Sources and Remarks

The most important book on the general economic conditions and trends of the period dealt with in Chapter III is Lenin's *Imperialism: The Highest Stage of Capitalism*. Labour conditions after the war are dealt with in an outstanding book by Allen Hutt, *The Condition of the Working Class in Britain*. On the problem of the distressed areas—created by the incapacity of monopoly capitalism to make use of the whole labour force even in times of relatively great trade activity, except in intensive preparation for war—Wal Hannington, *The Problem of the Distressed Areas* and Ellen Wilkinson's book *The Town that was Murdered*, are to be recommended.

The index of unproductivity is composed in the following way: unemployment figures were taken for the years 1880 to 1920 from the trade union statistics, published in the *Abstract of Labour Statistics of the United Kingdom*; for the years 1921 to 1939 from the *Ministry of Labour Gazette*, January 1940; inroads in labour force through over-employment of unproductive forces

* Unreliable figure; general strike.   † First half of the year.

were computed by taking the adjusted census figures given in Bowley, *Wages and Income in the United Kingdom since 1860*, pp. 128-9, for all occupied persons except workers and farmers, and comparing the growth of this group with that of the working class; I then constructed an index of the growth of the first group of people assuming that they had grown at the rate the working class has grown, and the difference between the actual growth and this constructed growth was taken as the element of parasitism and decay; I assumed that between the census years the rate of growth in each group was annually the same; the percentage of national income spent on armaments was computed by comparing the official budget data on armament expenditure (April to March) with the national income (calendar year). The national income was computed as follows: for the years 1880 to 1914 I used the figures given by Bowley in his above-mentioned book; the five-year averages were re-computed into yearly figures with the help of Bowley's earlier yearly estimate of the national income ("Tests of National Progress," *The Economic Journal*, 1904) and his annual wage bill estimates in the above-mentioned book; for the years 1924 to 1937 I used Colin Clark's estimates given in his books *National Income and Outlay* and *The Conditions of Economic Progress*. For the years 1915 to 1923 and 1938 and 1939 I made estimates myself, except for 1918, when I used an estimate given in *The Economist* (September 30, 1939). The following table gives the figures used as national income data:

ESTIMATES OF THE NATIONAL INCOME, 1880 TO 1939

(Thousand Million Pounds)

Year	Income	Year	Income	Year	Income	Year	Income
1880	1·090	1895	1·450	1910	1·980	1925	4·710
1881	1·130	1896	1·490	1911	2·060	1926	4·525
1882	1·175	1897	1·550	1912	2·150	1927	4·720
1883	1·175	1898	1·630	1913	2·220	1928	4·710
1884	1·155	1899	1·705	1914	2·250	1929	4·765
1885	1·135	1900	1·785	1915	2·800	1930	4·700
1886	1·165	1901	1·785	1916	2·500	1931	4·265
1887	1·200	1902	1·745	1917	4·500	1932	4·210
1888	1·275	1903	1·750	1918	5·500	1933	4·335
1889	1·340	1904	1·710	1919	6·000	1934	4·710

ESTIMATES OF THE NATIONAL INCOME, 1880 TO 1939—*continued*

(*Thousand Million Pounds*)

Year	Income	Year	Income	Year	Income	Year	Income
1890	1·360	1905	1··760	1920	6·500	1935	5·030
1891	1·370	1906	1·860	1921	4·500	1936	5·340
1892	1·355	1907	1·930	1922	4·000	1937	5·760
1893	1·365	1908	1·850	1923	4·200	1938	5·500
1894	1·405	1909	1·880	1924	4·375	1939	6·000

As sources for the rates of wages in individual industries I used for the years 1900 to 1921 the figures given in the *Abstract of Labour Statistics*; for the years 1921 to 1939 the figures given in the same source as well as the *Ministry of Labour Gazette* (for estimates for 1939 and 1940) and E. C. Ramsbottom, "The Course of Wage Rates in the United Kingdom, 1921–1934," *Journal of the Royal Statistical Society, 1935*; figures for later years are given in other issues of the same journal. Figures for 1940 estimated from the *London and Cambridge Economic Service Bulletins*.

The cost of living for the years 1900 to 1914 was computed on the basis of the figures given in the *Abstract of Labour Statistics* and assuming that rents increased up to 1904 by 0·1 shilling bi-annually, remained stable from 1905 to 1912, and increased again by 0·1 shilling in 1913 and 1914. For the following years I used the official cost of living index published in the *Abstract of Labour Statistics* and in *The Ministry of Labour Gazette*.

Social insurance contributions were estimated to amount to 1½ per cent for the years 1912 to 1920, to 5 per cent in 1921 to 1930 and 1936 to 1940, to 6 per cent in 1931 to 1935. Unemployment insurance benefits were estimated to be 40 per cent of the average wage losses suffered from unemployment during the years 1921 to 1930 and 1934 to 1940, and 35 per cent during the years 1931 to 1933.

The wage figures, if not otherwise noted, refer to the end of the year; the same holds true of the cost-of-living figures. Unemployment figures refer to the average for the whole year.

The index of productivity was computed by using the employment figures given by Bowley in his above-mentioned book, with estimates of my own for the years 1920 to 1923, and the official data given in *The Ministry of Labour Gazette* for the years 1937 to 1939. The production index used for the years 1880 to 1928 is that computed by Hoffmann, and for the years 1929 up to the first half of 1939 that of the Board of Trade.

As to the computation of relative wages and the share of capital, cf. sources and remarks to Chapter II. The figures used for the computation are:

(1900 = 100)

Cycles	Physical Volume of Industrial Production	Wholesale Prices	Retail Prices
1895–1903	97	89	96
1904–08	107	99	102
1909–14	117	108	108
1924–32	118	151	181

For the production figures I used the frequently mentioned index by Hoffmann; for wholesale prices, Sauerbeck's index and *The Statist*; for retail prices the cost-of-living index; for population data, the official census and the official yearly estimates; and for real wages, the data computed for this book.

The strike statistics are taken from the *Abstract of Labour Statistics* and from *The Ministry of Labour Gazette*.

Many data given in this chapter are of better quality than those in previous chapters, because the statistical apparatus of the Government has improved and because we have more material at our disposal. On the other hand, such data as those on the national income or the relative position of labour are nothing better than very rough approximations. Many important data are altogether missing, especially studies on industrial fatigue and the general question of the increase in the intensity of work. Special studies, based on the material of a single factory or even only a department of a factory, are of no general use, especially as they do no more than confirm what we already know: that intensity of labour has increased universally and considerably.

CHAPTER IV

LABOUR CONDITIONS DURING TWO WARS

IT is instructive to study the development of labour conditions since 1939 not only by comparing them with pre-war conditions but also, and chiefly, by comparing them with the development of labour conditions during the last war.

War always brings a deterioration of labour conditions. Naturally, if an increasing amount of work and raw materials and machines is being spent on armaments, less and less is being left over for the production of "peace time goods," and if more and more has to go to a growing army with its altogether different standards of spending and consumption not only of arms, but also of consumption goods, then relatively less and less is left for the individual civilian consumer. This is true everywhere and in every big war; it is true to-day in the Socialist Soviet Union as well as in monopolist-capitalist Britain; it is true to-day when Britain wages a just war as it was true in 1914–1918 when she was waging a typical imperialist war.

But if we were only to investigate the question whether the standard of living and working of the British worker had deteriorated as compared with pre-war years, then we would not need to start a new chapter; a footnote, contested only by a few, would be quite sufficient. What we want to investigate in the following pages is not this question, but the amount of deterioration, the aspects of deterioration—and also certain aspects of an improvement of working and living conditions—and finally the changes brought about by the present war as compared with the previous one.*

1. WAGES AND PURCHASING POWER

The first and most important individual factor we shall investigate are wages and their purchasing power. Let us begin with

* I shall make much use for the study of present-day labour conditions of a pamphlet which Miss M. Heinemann wrote with me on the subject and which was published in the United States under the title: *British Workers in the War.*

wage rates. According to the computations of the Ministry of Labour and Professor A. L. Bowley, wage rates have developed as follows*—the choice of the dates in the following table will be obvious if we realize that for these dates we also have statistics of actual earnings:

WAGE RATES, 1938 TO 1943

(*October 1938 = 100*)

Date	Index
October, 1938	100
July, 1940	110½
July, 1941	118
January, 1942	122
July, 1942	124
January, 1943	126½
July, 1943	130

During the first nine months of the war wage rates increased by just about 10 per cent;† during the succeeding twelve months they rose by roughly 7 per cent, and during the eighteen months after that the rise was again only 7 per cent; since then the rise has been smaller still. That is, the war started with an average rise in wages of about 1 per cent per month; the rate then slowed down to little more than ½ per cent per month, and subsequently slowed down still further to little more than one-third of 1 per cent per month. How different were conditions during the previous war! Professor Bowley gives the following figures on wage rate increases at that time.‡

WAGE RATES, 1914 TO 1918

(*July 1914 = 100*)

Date	Index
July, 1914	100
July, 1915	105 to 110
July, 1916	115 to 120
July, 1917	135 to 140
July, 1918	175 to 180

Here we can observe just the opposite tendency. The rate of increase of the wage rate was slightly less at the beginning of the

* Cf. *Bulletin of the Institute of Statistics*, Oxford, vol. 6, No. 7.

† The index figure for August, 1939, is 100½; cf. *London and Cambridge Economic Service*, August 23, 1939.

‡ See A. L. Bowley, *Prices and Wages in the United Kingdom, 1914–1920*, Carnegie Endowment for International Peace, Economic and Social History of the World War, British Series; Oxford, 1921; p. 106.

war than in 1939–40—but then, instead of diminishing as during the present war, it increased from year to year, until in the year from July, 1917 to 1918 it reached about 2½ per cent per month.

The conclusion we can draw from this is that during the present war the rate of wages moved considerably less, was more stable than during the last war, and has tended during the course of the war to become more stable, whereas in the previous war it had the tendency to become more unstable.

But wages are only a very inadequate expression of what the worker brings home in his pay envelope. Let us first compare the wage rates and the gross earnings of the worker.*

EARNINGS OF WORKERS, 1938 TO 1943

Date	Index
October, 1938	100
July, 1940	130
July, 1941	142½
January, 1942	146
July, 1942	160
January, 1943	165
July, 1943	176

If we compare the development of earnings and that of wage rates we seem to be dealing with the working class of two very different countries. Earnings show a rise between two and three times as high as rates. There has been a continued rise in the earnings of the workers. How is this to be explained? Why have earnings and wage rates moved so differently? And how does the rise in earnings during the present war compare with that during the previous one? To answer the last question first: we have no exact data on the development of earnings during the last war; but everything goes to indicate that earnings rose more than during the present war, although we cannot be sure that the relative rise—relative to the rates—was as high as during the present war.

The rise in earnings above rates is due to various causes. Firstly, there is the fact that the number of hours worked has increased as compared with 1938, bringing short-time work up

* See, *Institute of Statistics*, Oxford, Bulletin, Vol. 5, No. 12, where Mr. J. L. Nicholson has published one of his many articles on wages, which become statistically better and socially more useful with every new issue of the Bulletin dealing with the subject, and Vol. 6, No. 7.

to full time work, and adding overtime work to full-time work. Secondly, overtime is paid relatively higher than normal time, and often special bonuses paid are included in the earnings, but not in the rates. Thirdly, workers have been shifted from low-paying industries to less low-paying ones, for instance from the textile industries to the engineering industries. One factor must be mentioned which makes for a decline of earnings relative to wage rates, and that is the increase in the number of women workers as compared with men.* But this latter factor does not play any serious role—Nicholson estimates its effect over the whole period from October, 1938, to July, 1943, at about 2 per cent. There are two reasons for the surprisingly small influence of this factor: the one is that the percentage of female wage earners has, in spite of the general growth in the employment of women, not increased very much, and secondly (less important) that average wages of women and especially of juveniles have risen more than those of men. In fact, the influence of the different sex-age group composition of the working force in industry is so small that I shall completely ignore it in the following table which gives a survey of the actual percentage influence of the various factors upon the increase of earnings:

IMPORTANCE OF VARIOUS CAUSES FOR THE RISE IN
EARNINGS, 1938 TO 1943

Period Ending	Rise due to Increase of Wage Rates Per cent	Rise due to Shifts between Industries† Per cent	Rise due to Overtime and Special Bonuses, etc. Per cent
October, 1938	0	0	0
July, 1940	10½	4	14
July, 1941	18	2	18
January, 1942	22	4	16
July, 1942	24	4	24
January, 1943	26½	6	23
July, 1943	30	8	25

During the first year of the war it was the increase in the hours of work and special bonuses which had the greatest influence in

* The percentage of juvenile workers employed has probably declined slightly and this has an effect on average wages contrary to that of the increased percentage of women employed—but the effect is almost nil during the years under review.

† Underestimates, as the figures are somewhat depressed by including the decline due to changes in the sex-age composition of the workers.

raising earnings. Up to July, 1941, the influence of the rise in wage rates and that of the rise in the number of hours worked, etc., was about equally great. During the following year, up to July, 1942, the weight of the influence of these two factors was fluctuating but about equally important. Since then the rise in wage rates has again won increasing influence. For July, 1943, Nicholson gives the following exact percentages, taking into account the influence of the changes in the sex-age composition of the working force:

Increase of Average Earnings	75·7 per cent
Due to rise in wage rates..	30·0 per cent
Due to overtime, etc.	27·3 per cent
Due to shifts between industries	7·8 per cent
Decline due to change in sex-age composition..	1·5 per cent

If we investigate the development of wages by age and sex we have again to be satisfied with a few indications as to the course of the development during the previous war, while we have satisfactory material for the present war.

AVERAGE EARNINGS BY AGE AND SEX, 1938 TO 1943*

Year and Month	Men		Youths and Boys (below 21 years)		Women		Girls (below 18 years)		All Workers	
	s.	d.	s.	d.	s.	d.	s.	d.	s.	d.
October, 1938	69	0	26	1	32	6	18	6	53	3
July, 1940	89	0	35	1	38	11	22	4	69	2
July, 1941	99	5	41	11	43	11	25	0	75	10
January, 1942	102	0	42	6	47	6	26	10	77	9
July, 1942	111	5	46	2	54	2	30	3	85	2
January, 1943	113	9	45	1	58	6	32	1	87	11
July, 1943	121	3	47	2	62	2	33	10	93	7

AVERAGE EARNINGS BY AGE AND SEX, 1938 TO 1943*
(October, 1938 = 100)

Year and Month	Men	Youths and Boys	Women	Girls	All Workers
October, 1938	100	100	100	100	100
July, 1940	129·0	134·5	119·7	120·7	129·9
July, 1941	144·1	160·7	135·1	135·1	142·4
January, 1942	147·8	162·9	146·2	145·2	146·0
July, 1942	161·5	177·0	166·7	163·5	159·9
January, 1943	164·9	172·8	180·0	173·4	165·1
July, 1943	175·7	180·8	191·3	182·9	175·7

* Cf. *Ministry of Labour Gazette*, February, 1944.

The highest increase in earnings was that for women aged eighteen and over, while wages for men increased least; the wages of boys and girls increased about equally. And yet, it is surprising, not that the wages of women rose more than those of men, but that they rose by so little more, for in October, 1938, women's wages were slightly less than half men's wages, and in 1943 they were only slightly more than half men's wages. Even this rise in women's wages is still exaggerated because a considerable part of the lessening of the difference between the wages of women and those of men is due to a shifting of the women to industries which always have paid higher wages to women—if they employed women at all. If we leave out of account the shifting within industry as a whole, then we find that the wages of women have not increased most, that they have increased relatively less than those of boys and girls, that they have increased almost exactly as much as those of men—the slight difference in favour of women making almost no difference at all. This shows that *the situation of women in industry has actually not changed at all*. The small number of women (among the many who do a man's work) who get the wage for the job and not the wage for the sex hardly count. *This is a very serious matter for women as well as for the whole working class.* For this means not only dilution—a matter of urgent necessity if we want to win the war as quickly as possible—but it makes for *disintegration of the wage structure, it makes dilution not a matter of progress but inoculates it with elements of retrogression*. The more the working class must be in favour of dilution of the job and of the working process if it makes for more efficiency in the struggle against Fascism, the more watchful the working class must be against the disintegration of the wage structure which has taken place during the present war.

And what is even more serious is the fact that, according to all evidence, we have this dilution of the wage structure taking place to a greater degree than during the last war. During the war of 1914–1918, from which the working class had nothing to gain, the wage structure became less corroded than during the present one. According to the material assembled by Bowley* we get the impression that during the last war the wages of women rose very much more than those of men. If we look at the wages

* L.c., chap. xv.

controlled by Trade Boards we find that the rates of men rose between July, 1914 and July, 1918 by 18 to 33 per cent, while those of women rose between 33 and 58 per cent.

If we investigate the development of wages of juveniles we find that they have experienced a genuine relative increase of wages, definitely not so insignificant as that of women. Their relative earnings have risen within the same industry by roughly 20 per cent more than those of men—the latter having risen since October, 1938, by about 64 per cent, while those of boys and girls have risen by 73 and 76 respectively. No reliable data for the last war are available for the purposes of comparison.

There is, however, one further factor which we must take into account: the difference in the increase in the number of hours worked by men and women. The working day of men has increased more than that of women between October, 1938, and July, 1943. This leads to a relative increase of weekly wages of men for two reasons: more hours of work, and more hours paid at overtime rates. Looking upon wages from the point of view of "the rate for the job," both facts make the position of women appear more unfavourable than it actually is. This is, however, not sufficient to invalidate our above statement on the relatively unfavourable development of the wages of women, especially as we have not taken into account the fact that women have, within the same industry, taken on more skilled work.

*   *   *

Up to now we have dealt only with money wages.* How have

* One critic of the manuscript to whom I owe much remarked on the lengthy treatment of money wages: "I don't like the very detached treatment of money wages and earnings before you deal with prices. I don't see that in relation to last war the figures mean anything till you know what was happening to prices." This is a most interesting comment as it shows a very serious under-estimate of the information which money wages can give us. Apart from the information we extracted on the development, for instance, of the wages of men and women, one should realize the following important fact: if real wages remain stable, this may either be due to stability of money wages and prices (which happens quite often) or it may be due to the fact that money wages rose just as much as prices, a rare occurrence and usually indicating a considerable strength of the labour movement. This example alone should be sufficient to prove the importance of a careful study of money wages by themselves.

wages developed as compared with the cost of living? The official cost of living index has during the period under review developed as follows:

THE COST OF LIVING, 1938 TO 1943

Year and Month*	Index
October, 1938	100
July, 1940	121
July, 1941	128
January, 1942	129
July, 1942	129
January, 1943	128
July, 1943	129

· The cost of living rose considerably during the first nine months of the war (in August, 1939, the index was exactly the same as in October, 1938); during the following twelve months it rose only slightly, and then remained about stable. Such stability during many years of war is not only surprising but favours the working class in so far as it facilitates for them the task of watching over the development of real wages. And such a development is very different from that which occurred in the previous war when the cost of living index moved as follows :†

THE COST OF LIVING, 1914 TO 1918

Year and Month	Index
July, 1914	100
July, 1915	125
July, 1916	145
July, 1917	180
July, 1918	205

During the first year of war the cost of living moved very similarly, both in 1914–1915 and in 1939–1940—it increased between one-fifth and one-quarter. But then a very great difference set in. Although in the case of the previous war the rate of increase of the first war year (1914–1915) is not maintained in the second, it is equalled in the third, and in the fourth war year the cost of living rose to twice the height it had reached in 1914, while in 1943 it is, as in the preceding years, somewhat less than 30 per cent above the August, 1939, level.

But—one is almost inclined to say "of course," as the official cost of living indices are at all times a subject difficult to approach without biting criticism—the official cost of living index is not

* 1st of the month.   † Bowley, l.c. p. 106.

an accurate reflection of the course of prices of the goods which the worker buys. This is no original statement—even the Ministry of Labour which computes the index remarks: "no allowance being made for any changes in the standard of living since that date" (August, 1914!—J. K.), "or for any economies or readjustments in consumption and expenditure since the outbreak of the war" (this means the present war.—J. K.).*

That the official index was already inadequate during the last war was obvious to many even then, and so some tried to make corrections. It is typical of the state of labour statistics (political as well as technical) that the only "serious" attempt to correct the official index was that of Professor Bowley,† and that he came to the conclusion that the cost of living for the workers had risen less than was officially assumed. He argued that the worker could not buy many things in the quantities in which he could buy them in peace time, and thus the quantities were cut down by Bowley with very slight additions for other goods. Consequently the index of the cost of living, as computed by Bowley, increased considerably less than the official index, while in reality the cost of living for the workers increased more than the official index. It is all the more interesting that under the guidance of Professor Bowley the Oxford Institute of Statistics is trying to compute an improved cost of living index which shows during the present war an increase in the cost of living greater than that of the official index—a sign that it approaches reality in contrast to the escape from reality a quarter of a century ago. The actual computations of the corrected cost of living index during the present war were made by J. L. Nicholson, who makes the following criticism of what he regards as the chief shortcomings of the official index:‡

"The Ministry of Labour's cost of living index, during this period, suffers from two main deficiencies. On the one hand subsidies have been mainly applied to foods which are included in the index; and particularly, it appears, to foods which are overweighted in comparison with their relative importance in general expenditure. On the other hand, indirect taxes have

---

* Always put into the monthly statement in the *Ministry of Labour Gazette* on the development of the cost of living.

† L.c. chap. iv.

‡ L.c. vol. 4, No. 17.

been imposed on tobacco and drink which are not adequately represented in the index. As a consequence, the index fails to give an accurate reflection of the general price level."

Nicholson has tried to correct these faults, and gives the following comparison of the official and his corrected index:*

THE COST OF LIVING, 1938 TO 1942

	Index	
Year and Month	Official	Revised
October, 1938	100	100
July, 1940	119	120
July, 1941	127½	133
October, 1942	128	140

These figures give a very different picture from that in the previous table. They show that instead of remaining about stable —as the official cost of living index indicated—prices have gone up continuously from year to year. And the increase up to the present has by no means been negligible, even after the serious rise in the first year of the war. Yet, this corrected table also indicates a fundamental difference between the development of the cost of living in this war and the last: the rate of increase was, during the last war, not exceptional during the first war year, and it did not show a decided tendency to become smaller, being for instance between July, 1916, and July, 1917, roughly the same as between July, 1914, and July, 1915; during the present war, however, also according to the revised figures of Nicholson, the rate of increase has had a tendency to decline, in fact it has declined by roughly half from year to year up to the present time. If we adjust the most recent computations by Nicholson† for the periods for which we have data on earnings, we get the following index of the cost of living during the present war:

COST OF LIVING, 1938 TO 1943

	Index	
Year and Month	Official	Revised
October, 1938	100	100
July, 1940	119	120
July, 1941	128	136
January, 1942	129	138
July, 1942	129	143
January, 1943	128	145
July, 1943	129	150

* L.c. vol. 4, No. 17.   † L.c. vol. 6, No. 10.

If we now compare average actual earnings with the revised cost of living index, we arrive at the following result:

MONEY EARNINGS, COST OF LIVING AND REAL WAGES, 1938 TO 1943

(1938 = 100)

Year and Month	Money Earnings	Cost of Living	Real Wages
October, 1938	100	100	100
July, 1940	130	120	108
July, 1941	142	136	104
January, 1942	146	138	106
July, 1942	160	143	112
January, 1943	165	145	114
July, 1943	176	150	117

From this table we get the impression that real wages have increased not inconsiderably during the war. In 1943 they were, according to this table, about one-sixth higher than before the war. But we have up to now neglected one most important factor which nobody has taken into account when computing a cost of living index, and that is the enormous increase in direct taxation. Curiously enough, taxes seem to be regarded as expenditure of the worker to be met by him without any inroad into his expense budget. Mr. Nicholson estimates* that direct taxation of wages before the war did not play any role, that direct wage deductions amounted to about 3 per cent of earnings in 1940, and 7 per cent in 1941. If we use the figures he gives in another study for the total wage bill and the figures of income tax liabilities and social insurance contributions,† we arrive at the following deductions which must be made for additional direct taxes and additional social insurance contributions:‡

1940	2 per cent
1941	6 per cent
1942	8 per cent
1943	9 per cent

If we apply these deductions we arrive at the following development of real wages:

* *Bulletin*, vol. 4, No. 17. † *Bulletin*, vol. 6, No. 10.
‡ The percentage varies sometimes considerably over the year—before and after the new budget. It is very much higher for skilled unmarried workers—so high in fact, that their payment, before the pay-as-you-earn legislation, often left them for many months in a very precarious position.

NET REAL WAGES, 1938 TO 1943

Year and Month	Net Real Wages
October, 1938	100
July, 1940	106
July, 1941	98
July, 1942	103
January, 1943	104
July, 1943	106

These figures look quite different from those given in the previous table: they indicate that net real wages have fluctuated not inconsiderably from year to year, that in 1941 they were about 2 per cent below 1938, and in the other years between 3 and 6 per cent above the 1938 level. But even these figures are still too high—only nobody knows by how much. Nicholson has made some estimates of the increase in the cost of living due to rationing and shortages and used highly ingenious methods to arrive at such estimates. But I do not think that he has been successful in measuring the effects of rationing and shortages. While it is truly impossible to go further in bringing real wages nearer to reality in terms of figures, it is necessary to mention these factors (rationing and shortages) in order to make it clear that real wages—because of the shortage in housing alone,* I would say—are below the 1938 level.

But while it is not possible to compute actual net real wages, while we must content ourselves with the statement that real wages are somewhat below the 1938 level, this already is a very significant fact. During the war 1914–1918 the situation was different, as the following table will show:†

WAGES AND COST OF LIVING, 1914 TO 1918

Year and Month	Wage Rates	Cost of Living
July, 1914	100	100
July, 1915	105 to 110	125
July, 1916	115 to 120	145
July, 1917	135 to 140	180
July, 1918	175 to 180	205

While it is true that the wage index is an index of rates and not of earnings, it is equally true that the cost of living index is

* Rents have officially not increased, but the actual prices which the workers in blitzed or over-crowded quickly grown armament towns have to pay are sometimes very considerably above those paid in 1938, especially since the prices for furnished rooms are not controlled.

† Bowley, l.c. p. 106.

the official one, and therefore absolutely inadequate in showing the real rise in the cost of living. And while Nicholson* with his formula arrives at a decline of average net real wages below the 1938 level of 4 per cent in 1940, of 11 per cent in 1941 and of 6 per cent in 1942—it is obvious to all students of labour conditions that real wages in the previous war declined more than they have done during the present war. While real wages have also declined during the present war, this decline has been smaller than during the last war.

In conclusion one can summarize the development of real wages:

The real value of what the worker got from his work and could actually use for his living was smaller during the war than before the war; there is no evidence that the decline in the real value continued after 1941; on the contrary, it is not improbable that the summer of 1941 is up to now the lowest point in real wages for the workers. While real wages have declined as compared with the pre-war years, they have not declined as much as during the last war.

*   *   *

There remain, however, two important questions to be answered: how do actual wages compare with the actual cost of living? Wages may decline from a standard which assures a decent and healthy life, and they may decline from a standard which is below such a level—and, furthermore, real wages, during a war, may change slightly, and the actual standard of life may change considerably because of considerable changes in the amount and quality of goods available for consumption.

The Labour Research Department has made a valuable attempt to compute a cost of living minimum† "to enable us to assess the wage necessary for physical efficiency," as B. Seebohm Rowntree formulates it.‡ The Labour Research Department arrives, for April, 1942, at a minimum of 100s. per week which is needed for the British war worker (with his long hours of work and doing heavy work) to raise a family with three children. This is, by the Labour Research Department, rightly called a

* *Bulletin*, vol. 5, No. 7.
† See *Wages in 1942, Facts and Figures for Trade Unionists*, published by Labour Research Department.
‡ *The Human Needs of Labour.*

"rock-bottom minimum standard." If we add to this the increase in the cost of living between April, 1942 and the average for 1943, we arrive for 1943 at a cost of living minimum of about 105s. per week.

If we now compare the average wages of men in various industries, as published in the *Ministry of Labour Gazette** with this minimum, then we find that the following industries paid, on the average, a worker sufficient to raise a family with three children on his own earnings:

> Treatment of non-metalliferrous mine and quarry products
> Chemical, paint, oil, etc.
> Metal, engineering and shipbuilding
> Paper, printing, stationery, etc.
> Building, contracting, etc.
> Government industrial establishments

In the following industries the wages of adult male workers reached 80 to 99 per cent of the minimum:

> Brick, pottery and glass
> Textiles
> Leather, fur, etc.
> Clothing
> Food, drink and tobacco
> Woodworking
> Transport, storage, etc. (excl. railways)
> Mining†
> Public utility services

In the following industries the wages reached less than 80 per cent of the minimum:

> Agriculture†
> Public utility services‡

Only four large industries reached or passed the existence minimum for a family. This does not mean that only the workers in these industries could live on the minimum standard. For

---

* June, 1943, and February, 1944.
† Not included in the Ministry's survey.   ‡ Beginning of 1943.

firstly, there are many workers who have no family or a family with less than three children; secondly, there are many workers' families where not only the husband but also the wife earns something and perhaps also the children. Nor does it mean that all workers in these industries can live on this minimum, because a good number of them have more than three children or other dependants. Moreover, the above wage-existence minimum relations refer to each of these industries as a whole but not to all individual branches. In the paper, printing, etc., industries only one of the four individual branches into which this group is subdivided by the Ministry paid, early in 1943, the existence minimum: printing, publishing and bookbinding.

On the other hand, in a number of other industries which on the average pay less than the minimum, there are some branches which pay more than the minimum—but not many! There are in July, 1943, three, for instance, in the textile industry and in food, drink and tobacco, two in clothing, one in leather, etc.

On the whole, it can be said, that the great majority of the workers have to live below the minimum if only the husband earns and the family consists of man, wife and three or more children. And, it should be added, if all the circumstances are taken into account—the wife working, a smaller number of children in many families, etc.—even then the majority of the working people live to-day below this minimum. That is, the working class is not able to restore fully its own working strength and to rear a new generation which will be healthy, and later to work with full strength. Wholly satisfactory conditions are not to be expected during a war. Conditions were probably worse during the last war. And conditions are, in this respect, undoubtedly worse, for instance, in the Soviet Union to-day. The decisive question for the present rather is: are the means of living available to-day distributed in such a way that those who need them most get most? This must be clearly denied. *The workers doing heavy and very heavy work in 1943 are much less well nourished than the food-stuffs available would warrant. There can be no doubt that in respect of food, the German miner, for instance, is better off in 1943 than the British miner, with serious consequences for the relative coal output in the two countries, that is, for our fight against Fascism.*

*　　　　*　　　　*

Under war conditions it is possible that a considerable section of the working class do not spend the whole of their earnings, but save part of them for patriotic reasons. That is, the development of real wages does not fully reflect the development of the standard of living of the workers. While it is not possible to compute exact figures of working class consumption, it is advisable to study in this connection the computations by J. L. Nicholson* for the development of consumption of the whole of the population. Nicholson's figures are based on the best source available, the Government White Paper, "An Analysis of the Sources of War Finance and an Estimate of the National Income and Expenditure in 1938, 1940, 1941 and 1942." The index numbers of consumption, according to these sources, have developed as follows:

CONSUMPTION
(*1938 = 100*)

Categories	1940	1941	1942	1943†
Food	88	83½	86	80
Drink and Tobacco ..	98	104	103	103
Rent	103	102	101	101
Fuel and Light ..	93	96	96	92
Clothing	85	61	59	60
Remaining Items ..	78	70	69	66
Total Consumption	88	82	82	79

Nicholson then goes on to make a somewhat "hypothetical adjustment" for the effects of rationing and shortages and arrives at the following final index of total consumption:

TOTAL CONSUMPTION, 1938 TO 1943

Year	Index
1938	100
1940	86
1941	79
1942	79
1943†	76

Consumption has, thus, declined by about one quarter since 1938. It has declined more for the skilled than for the unskilled and more for the employed than for the formerly unemployed workers—in fact for the last-named consumption has undoubtedly

* *Bulletin*, vol. 5, No. 10, and No. 14.   † My estimate.

increased; it has declined most in the case of all those who receive to-day the same pension or benefit as before the war, or only very little more, such as the aged workers, the invalids of labour, and so on. It is doubtful whether consumption of clothing has fallen as much for the workers as the above figures indicate, as rationing has undoubtedly cut much deeper into the clothing budget of the rich. The same holds true, perhaps, for food, but in this case the difference between the decline indicated in the above table and the actual decline cannot have been very great. In a number of respects the decline has been considerably greater than the above tables indicate: usually due to a deterioration in the quality of goods which is not reflected in the above tables.

In conclusion we can say: the standard of living of the workers has declined for the average of all workers during the present war; the section of the workers who live better to-day than before the war are the formerly unemployed workers, and many workers where more family members are working than before the war, a total of at least three to four millions.

The standard of living of the workers has declined less during the present war than during the preceding war.

While a decline of the standard of living is to be expected in every country engaged in a big war—whether the war is a predatory or a just one—the decline can be distributed over the whole population, and more specifically over the working class, either in a progressive or in a reactionary way. *There can be no doubt that the distribution of available goods is better to-day after four years of war than either at the beginning of the present war or than during the whole course of the last war. At the same time it must be pointed out that conditions are by no means as well as they could be, that there are still sections of the population who get much more than corresponds to their share in the war effort, and there are some sections among the workers who, as measured by their especially hard work (miners, blast-furnacemen, etc.), get considerably less than they ought to, on the basis of the means of living available. To those who get less than they ought to, on the basis of the means available, must be added the aged and the invalids of labour.*

2. EMPLOYMENT AND UNEMPLOYMENT

One of the most difficult tasks in a war is the distribution of man-power between the armed forces and the industries providing them with weapons, and between the industries producing goods necessary for the upkeep of the working strength of man-power and the industries providing the weapons. Formerly, when wars were "less total," this problem did not play a great role, as the nation's effort spent on the war either was very much smaller than to-day or—as for instance in the wars of the Revolution on the French side (end of the eighteenth century)—the amount of weapons needed by an army was not very great as measured by the working power of a nation. The problem became real and serious only during the last war, and in the present war all countries have acted on the basis of experience gained during the last war.

The direction of man-power requires a very considerable restriction of the personal freedom of movement of the individual worker. While during the last war the first serious inroads into this freedom of the civilian worker were made only in July, 1915 (The Munitions of War Act, 1915), the first measures of importance in the present war were taken at once, and by June, 1940, that is nine months after the beginning of the war, many of the most important man-power measures had been taken. The measures taken in 1939 and 1940 referred not only to the freedom of movement of the civilian worker, but also to the right of the worker to work in a certain industry and to the right of a person engaged otherwise than as a wage earner to continue in his profession. That is, the civilian could henceforth be ordered to any kind of work, whatever and wherever the job.

In the following we shall see how the composition of the working force of the nation changed during the last and during the present war. *

Britain entered the war in 1939 with about 16 million wage

* For the development during the war 1914–1918 see, apart from such official publications as *The Board of Trade Journal* (especially March 6, 1919) and the *Abstract of Labour Statistics of the United Kingdom*, Humbert Wolfe, *Labour Supply and Regulation, Carnegie Endowment for International Peace, Economic and Social History of the World War*, British Series, Oxford, 1923.

and salary earners, usually employed full time. But not all of them were actually able to work:

Unemployed before the war	..	..	1,500,000
Sick before the war	..	..	..	500,000
On strike	..	..	..	..	37,000

Total number of workers not employed 2,000,000

The total active labour force with which Britain entered the present war, therefore, was around 14 millions, of whom roughly 4·2 millions were women. But these figures do not give the total population which could be mobilized for work of some kind. While the male population between the ages of 14 and 64 was to a very large extent occupied, the women were occupied full-time, if we exclude in this connection the performance of home duties by housewives, to little more than one-third—about 6·5 million women out of somewhat less than 17 millions being occupied.

The chief reserve of new man power for the war were the women. A further very important source was the re-distribution of man-power actually already somehow employed; a third important source was the employment of younger people and the retention of older people. Finally, a very important additional source was the lengthening of the working day. Through intensive as well as extensive methods the working power could be increased very considerably. And then, there is one further source of man-power which cannot be over-estimated in its importance, and which, in many respects, is playing in the Soviet Union perhaps the greatest role: and that is the increased performance per worker because of his interest in the war effort. This interest may objectively conflict with his own real interest as it did in the first period of war enthusiasm of the misguided workers of the war of 1914–1918, or it may correspond to his real interest as it does to-day in the allied countries. But whether it is misguided or not, its importance is very great, and if it corresponds to his real interests it is not only great but sustained.

Let us study in more detail what results the various methods of recruiting man-power have had during the present war as far as this can be done under the statistical blackout, and the additional handicap of dealing in part with matters which can be measured

* Including domestic service, etc.

only with the greatest difficulty even under ideal conditions.

The absorption of the unemployed was relatively slow at first. This was due largely to inefficient handling during the first months of the war of the problems involved. In July, 1939, there were a number of people unemployed who were no longer counted officially as unemployed, but who in the course of the war found work. I have estimated them as roughly 200,000 in July, 1939, giving above an unemployment figure of 1·5 millions as compared with the official one of 1,326,134 for Britain (Great Britain and Northern Ireland). It is highly probable that their number declined more slowly than that of the officially recognized unemployed. If the official statistics indicate a decline of unemployment from 1·33 million in July, 1939, to 775,000 in December, 1940, unemployment had in fact probably declined even less. Thus, the number of unemployed declined even less than the official figures indicate, and even the official figure at the end of 1940 was still too high to speak of a serious and successful effort on the part of the Government to cope with unemployment. It was only in the second half of 1941 that it could be said that unemployment had reached a level commensurate with a serious war effort in the direction of man-power. By the end of 1941 the total number of unemployed was little over 200,000, and one year later it was around 100,000.

During the last war, the absorption of the unemployed was much quicker at first than during the present war—unemployment before the outbreak of the war being considerably lower than before the outbreak of the present war: 3·6 per cent in July, 1914, as compared with 8·5 per cent in August, 1939.* During the second half of 1915 the percentage of unemployment had declined to 0·9, one quarter of the pre-war level, while by the end of 1940 it had declined by only half. In the course of 1916 unemployment again declined by almost 50 per cent in the previous war, reaching a percentage of 0·5 in the second half of 1916; that trend had reached its full extent; it did not decline further in the course of that war. During the present war, the chief effort in drawing the unemployed into the war effort was

* These figures are not strictly comparable; but they are sufficient for purposes of a rough comparison.

made only in 1941, and the decline in unemployment continued during 1942 and 1943, while in 1917 and in 1918 unemployment was around the 1916 level.

*   *   *

The employment of women has increased not inconsiderably during the present war—just as during the previous one. Wolfe* estimates that the total number of women drawn into work on the civilian side from 1914 to 1918 was over 1,500,000. But he does not cover all occupations. As the number of domestics, for instance, declined, it is more probable that the total number of women additionally mobilized for work in civilian occupations increased only from 5·0 to 6·3 millions.† The number of women serving in the army was relatively small—less than 100,000. How many more women are to-day employed on the home front than in 1939?‡ No official statistics have been published. But from occasional ministerial speeches one gets the definite impression that their number is less than 2,000,000. *That is, the number of women additionally employed in civil occupations to-day is probably not much greater than during the last war.* How is this to be explained?

The total number of women employed as wage or salary earners outside domestic service in July, 1914, can be estimated at rather more than three and a quarter millions, as compared with roughly five millions in July, 1918. To this must be added the relatively small number of women employed by the military authorities. The total number of women employed in July, 1939, as salary and wage earners outside domestic service was about four and a quarter millions, and to-day it is at best six and a quarter millions. The difference in the number of women employed as wage and salary earners, especially if the growth of the population is taken into account, is not very great in the two wars. During the present war, however, many more women are employed by the military; one can estimate their number at more than half a million. But even this number is not a full gain over the last war, as then there were also some women

---

* L.c. p. 77.
† See also D. M. Barton, "The Course of Women's Wages," *Journal of the Royal Statistical Society*, July, 1919.
‡ In comparing conditions during the last and during the present war, the change in the age composition of the population does not play any serious role.

employed by the military authorities. On the whole, one can say, that Britain has mobilized about two and a half million women as wage and salary earners and for the military authorities,* in addition to the roughly four and a quarter million women employed during the last pre-war month. In the previous war the total additional mobilization of women power for these purposes was perhaps one and three-quarters of a million in addition to a pre-war women contingent of over three and a half millions. The total number of women working in such jobs is to-day, after more than four years of war, over seven millions as compared with over five after four years in the last war: undoubtedly an achievement. But the reservoir of man-power, presented by women, is still by no means exhausted. Given the necessary pre-requisites, such as crèches and more British restaurants or other forms of feeding the people without bothering every woman individually about it, the additional labour power to be gained from the women's reservoir can still be increased.†

The relative size of the additional amount of women-power mobilized in this war as compared with the last can be gauged by studying the percentage of women employed in important industries. Nicholson‡ has made, in this field of labour conditions too, a highly interesting study, giving for the middle of 1942 and 1938 comparative figures of employment in the industries covered by the regular wage surveys of the Ministry of Labour (that is all important industries, with the exception of mining, railways and agriculture). Before we study the general figures, it is interesting to study those for engineering, one of the most important war industries.

PERCENTAGE DISTRIBUTION OF WORKERS IN ENGINEERING INDUSTRIES

Period	Men	Youths	Women	Girls
July, 1938	$67\frac{1}{2}$	17	$11\frac{1}{2}$	4
July, 1942	63 to $61\frac{1}{4}$	16 to 12	15 to $22\frac{1}{2}$	6 to 4*

* Less those who left domestic service for other occupations.
† Although it must be realized that after a certain point has been reached in mobilizing women, the amount of woman power absorbed by crèches in relation to the number of women (with several children) freed for work is considerable.
‡ *Bulletin*, vol. 5, No. 5.

This table is immensely interesting. Firstly, it shows that *the percentage of men employed in engineering has changed very little as compared with pre-war years*: at most, it has declined from somewhat more than two-thirds to somewhat less than two-thirds. The percentage of women which was very small in 1938 has at best been doubled, increasing from 11½ to 22½ per cent.

From the study by Wolfe* we can get roughly comparable figures for the previous war. According to Wolfe the total number of people employed in engineering (called by him "metals, including engineering, etc.") was:

In 1914 1,804,000   In 1918 2,418,000

His figures for the employment of women in the same industry are:

170,000 in July, 1914   594,000 in July, 1918

From this we can compute the following percentage figures which we set beside those for 1938–1942, reckoning youths as men and girls as women:

EMPLOYMENT OF MEN AND WOMEN IN ENGINEERING
PERCENTAGES, 1914, 1918, 1938 AND 1942

Sex	1914	1918	1938	1942
Men	91	75	84½	79 to 73½
Women	9	25	15½	21 to 26½

The percentage of women employed in engineering before the war was somewhat greater in 1938 than in 1914; but in 1918, the percentage of women employed was about the same as in 1942. This must not, however, make us overlook the important fact that in 1944 women are doing much more complex and "men's" work than in 1918.†

If we compare conditions in industry as a whole we arrive at the following figures, using again the tables computed by Nicholson:

PERCENTAGES DISTRIBUTION OF WORKERS IN THE
PRINCIPAL INDUSTRIES

Period	Men	Youths	Women	Girls
July, 1938	59	14	21	6
July, 1942	57½ to 56½	14 to 10	22½ to 29	6 to 4½

* L.c. pp. 73 and 77.
† A fact of quite special significance when we remember the very unfavourable development of women's wages.

Again we find that the percentage of men employed in industry has changed very little; this time even less than in the specific industry investigated above. The percentage of women employed has not increased spectacularly. Probably less than one-third of the industrial workers are women—and if we take into account the fact that the above figures exclude mining, agriculture and the railways, we can say, that it is more than probable that of the total number of wage and salary earners in civilian occupations less than one-third are women, including girls.

If we compare the general civilian employment of women during the present and during the last war, we arrive at the following highly interesting table, covering the most important industries in this as well as in the last war:

PERCENTAGE DISTRIBUTION OF WORKERS IN THE PRINCIPAL
INDUSTRIES, 1914 TO 1918 AND 1938 TO 1942

Sex	1914	1918	1938	1942
Men	76	62	73	$71\frac{1}{2}$ to $66\frac{1}{2}$
Women	24	38	27	$28\frac{1}{2}$ to $33\frac{1}{2}$

Even though the mobilization of women was less intensive during the last war than during the present one the percentage of women employed in civilian work was greater at the end of the last war than it is to-day. This is due to the fact that to-day more women are doing military work, and more men have been retained in industry.

The above figures also give us some insight into the recruitment of juveniles. If we bear in mind that a considerable number of juveniles (men below the age of 21, and women below that of 18 years) have been absorbed by the military authorities, it is surprising that the above estimates by Nicholson indicate that possibly the percentage of young people has remained the same in industry, and that, if it has somewhat declined, the decline has been so small. No comparative figures are available for the last war, but it is very probable that the number and percentage of youth (male) kept in civilian occupations has been considerably greater during the present than during the last war, although the total civilian and military employment has been probably the same. As to girls, I should not hesitate to say that their combined military and civilian employment was more intense during the present than during the last war, and that during the present war the military authorities have obtained a very much greater share than during the last war. It is not possible to say that the percentage of girls employed in civilian occupations is higher during the present than during the last war as it is not possible, with the material available, to compare the effects of the greater comb-out generally during the present war with the effects of the greater military employment of girls. Even less do we know about the comparative absorption of old workers. Wolfe* estimates the number of older men who deferred retirement or who returned to work after retirement at 200,000 for 1914–1918. I would not be surprised if the number has been much greater during the present war, even if we take into account the fact that the absolute and relative number of older workers was larger before the present than before the last war.

The last important problem of man-power mobilization to be studied is that of the distribution over various industries. It is obvious that the maintenance of an adequate civilian army of workers can be really useful only if it is distributed in such a way that it best contributes to the war effort against Fascism. While we have very little information on this subject for the last war, we have some data to show the changes in distribution of man-power during the present war. Mr. M. Kalecki, of the Institute of Statistics, Oxford, has made some highly interesting computations in terms of "1938 workers."† Since his data include gain of man-power through a lengthened working day, the employment of 10 more "1938 men" in 1942 does not necessarily mean the employment of 10 more people; if all of them worked 10 per cent more hours, then an increase in the number of "1938 men" up to 1942 by 10 would mean only about 9 additional people employed. Keeping this in mind we find from Mr. Kalecki's tables that the total number of workers released from consumption goods industries was about 1½ millions up to 1941, and that by 1942 roughly 2 million workers had been released as compared with 1938 from civilian consumption goods producing industries. As, furthermore, general production for export declined rapidly, a further million workers could be released between 1938 and 1941; 1942 brought no new releases in this respect. Private

* L.c. p. 72.   † Bulletin, Vol. 5, No. 11.

investments (including those by local authorities) also declined
rapidly during the war, and released 2·5 million workers between
1939 and 1941; 1942 brought no new releases from this source.
*Thus, we can say that the war effort had gained through better employment
of available workers about 5 million workers by 1941, about 5½ million
workers by 1942, and about the same figure by 1943,* possibly rather
less than in 1942 because of a probable slight shortening of the
total number of hours worked. *No mean achievement and one which
is generally much too little appreciated in its importance.*

*   *   *

The total civilian employment of wage and salary earners
during the last war declined not inconsiderably during the first
year. Wolfe* gives the following figures of losses of the occupied
male population after one year of war:

LOSSES OF OCCUPIED POPULATION DURING THE FIRST YEAR IN THE LAST WAR

	Per cent		*Per cent*
Woollen and Worsted	12·5	Other metals ..	20·8
Small Arms ..	16·0	Coal, etc.	21·8
Shipbuilding	16·5	Cycle, etc.	22·3
Iron and Steel	18·8	Electrical Engineering	23·7
Engineering ..	19·5	Chemicals and Explosives	23·8
Wire-drawing, etc. ..	19·7		

Some of the losses in man-power were made good in the course
of the following years. But the total of man-power again declined
in 1916, made a slight gain in 1917, and was again smaller in
1918. As compared with July, 1914, man-power was smaller.

In July, 1915, by 819,000
In July, 1916, by 889,000
In July, 1917, by 842,000
In July, 1918, by 871,000

Total man-power in the principal industries was 13,886,000
in July, 1914, and 13,015,000 in 1918.

In this respect the situation is fundamentally different during
the present war. Drawing on the experience of man-power
shortage, especially in the most important war industries during
the previous war, the Government has watched out much more

* L.c. p. 14.

carefully during the present war, and has seen to it that there has been no depletion of civilian man-power. According to the estimates of Nicholson,* using methods developed by Kalecki, employment developed as follows:

TOTAL EMPLOYMENT, 1914 TO 1918 AND 1938 TO 1943

(1914 = 100) †		(1938 = 100)	
Year	Index	Year	Index
1914	100	1938	100
1915	94	1939‡	103
1916	94	1940	100½
1917	94	1941	105
1918	94	1942	106
		1943§	103

From this we see that after an initial drop which was so small that employment in 1940 was still higher than in 1938, the total number of people employed has increased slightly during the war up to 1942. If it is realized that this development took place while the number of men and women under arms increased from roughly half a million in 1939 to over 4 millions, then it must be said that the man-power effort of Britain—in spite of so many short-comings which are obvious from the preceding pages—has been a very considerable one, and that as far as the civilian man-power force is concerned, it has, on the whole, been managed and used, conserved in numbers and put to work, in a way appropriate to the enormous tasks which this war against Fascism has set us.

If we compare, for instance, the man-power effort of Britain with that of Germany, we can say: the military strength of the nation has been used to an infinitely smaller degree and with an infinitely smaller success for the right purposes, up to the first half of 1944, that is up to the invasion of the continent, than the German military man-power has been used for the most nefarious purposes; the civilian strength of Britain, however, has been used not only for a better purpose—that is obvious to everybody— but also with more intelligence and foresight—a fact which is not obvious to everybody. The recent debate on woman-power in the House of

* L.c. vol. 5, No. 7.
  † Computed on basis of figures given in the *Board of Trade Journal*, March 6, 1919.
  ‡ Cf. *Ministry of Labour Gazette*, January, 1940; figure refers to January–August.
  § My estimate.

Commons has shown that this has been done not without resistance from reactionary forces with vested interests not only in economic sources of wealth but also in a policy of too little and too late. Mobilization of civilian man-power and intelligent use of the forces available are—in marked contrast to military man-power and its use*—a field in which vested interests have been beaten, although it must not be overlooked that they still hold numerous outposts and nests which ought to be cleared up.

3. Hours of Work, Productivity and Accidents

Before the present war, a very large number of workers worked the eight-hour day, and the Factory Acts limited the working week for young workers under 16 to 44 hours. Before the war of 1914 the working day was longer, the majority of workers working at least nine hours per day. But as soon as the war started, in 1914 as well as in 1939, the hours of work per day and per week began to increase, and *by 1940 the working day was not different from that in 1915 in many factories, especially those concerned with the production of armaments and other goods necessary for the armed forces.* In the second half of 1940 many munition and other armament firms worked a 12-hour day or even longer. At the same time many firms did not only lengthen the working day but also the working week—during the previous war as well as during the present one. At that time a 72-hour week or a seven-day week were not unusual in many armament factories.

In fact, the number of hours worked rose so rapidly and so high that after some time, in 1941, the authorities had to intervene in the interest of output, accidents, and health, and to warn against the ill-effects of an unduly lengthened working day. In his report for 1940, the Chief Inspector of Factories† writes in his introductory letter, dated September, 1941 : "Experience of the year 1940 has shown that some valuable lessons of the last war had been widely forgotten or were not yet sufficiently appreciated, and has provided us with further guidance for the future. I have particularly in mind the lessons that excessive hours mean less production and that proper breaks and rest days

* Written before the invasion of the Continent.
† Annual Report of the Chief Inspector of Factories for the year 1940.

are of great importance from the production standpoint." If one compares this statement with the constantly reiterated statements by the authorities during the preceding war that there is no clearly recognizable connection between hours of work and work efficiency, one sees that official willingness to recognize certain well known facts—well known for about a century—pertaining to labour conditions has made some progress. *

But whether the effects of too long hours of work on productivity were recognized or not, during the present as well as during the last war, the number of hours worked per week began to decline in the third year of the war, in 1917 as well as in 1942. That is, it began to decline in those factories which had "gone all out," and had introduced the twelve-hour day and/or the seven-day week. The Chief Inspector, in his report for 1942, can write: "The Inspectors report that generally speaking the tendency during the year was towards the reduction of the weekly hours not only of women and young persons, but of adult men whose hours are not controlled by the Factories Act." This development for a more rational, more progressive use of manpower began already in the second half of 1941 and continued all through 1942. The decline in the number of such excessive hours and days worked continued on a smaller scale in 1943. This is due partly to the fact that some of the most serious excesses had already been remedied in 1942. In the case of youths and women workers, who often work shorter hours than men, the progress of the shortening of the working day can be observed from a study of special permissions for long hours of work given for juveniles and women.

The report of the Chief Inspector of Factories for 1941 says: "Out of about 10,000 factories which had emergency permissions to employ women and young persons over 16 either on a system of day and night shifts or for more than 48 hours a week on a

---

* The Annual Report of the Chief Inspector of Factories for 1917 says, for instance: "Little further evidence has been gained during the year as to the effects of overtime on output. The relation is very difficult to determine without close and prolonged inquiry, which it has been impossible for the Inspectors to undertake. There is much conflict of evidence in the reports that have been received." And two years later, the Chief Inspector's report still says: "The reports disclose wide differences of experience as to the effect on production of shorter hours" (report on hours of work in the 1919 Report of the Chief Inspector of Factories).

day shift, returns showed that early in 1942 the permitted hours were between 55 and 60 in rather less than half the cases. This proportion has since tended to decrease."

And the next report, for 1942, indicates further progress, saying that not slightly more than half of the permits, but "about 70 per cent were given for 55 hours or less."

The diminution of the working day in factories working exceedingly long hours does not necessarily mean, however, that the average length of the working day has declined. It is possible, for instance, that the number of workers whose working week is increased from, say, 48 to 54 hours is much greater than that whose working week has declined from 60 to 54 hours; in this case we would have an increase in the average length of the working day. Unfortunately we have no reliable data on the general length of the working day, whether for the previous or for the present war. Nicholson* has made an estimate (in my opinion too audacious) of the average lengthening of the working week:

AVERAGE WORKING TIME

Year	Index
1938	100
1940	105
1941	107
1942	109
1943	108†

From this it could be concluded that, on the average, the eight-hour day prevailing before the war has been replaced by the nine-hour day—although it is not improbable, even on the basis of the figures of Nicholson, that the eight-hour day has generally been replaced by the 9½-hour day, while a certain number of people have continued to work on the old eight-hour day basis, and some have been reduced in their working day, partly because of lack of business, partly because of lack of raw materials.

While in the second half of 1940 and during the first half of 1941 the working day in the armament industries was probably the same as in 1915 and 1916—though it was considerably lower in the non-armament

* L.c. vol. 6, No. 10.
† *The Ministry of Labour Gazette*, February, 1944; figures refer to July, 1943.

factories—in 1942 *and* 1943 *the working day was shorter also in the*
armament factories than in 1917 *and in* 1918.

*   *   *

There is extremely little evidence available on the development
of the productivity of the worker. What little there is, chiefly in
the reports of the Select Committee on National Expenditure,
suggests that the productivity per worker has gone down. This
was no continuous process. After Dunkirk hourly productivity
was going up for a short time and daily productivity for some
time longer (because of the lengthening of the working day);
during the visit of the Soviet Trade Union Delegation in January,
1942, productivity was going up per day and per hour; when
North Africa was invaded by the Allied troops, productivity was
going up, and the same happened after the invasion of Sicily.
But on the whole, over the period of four years of war, productivity has tended to decline. This has been due to a variety of
reasons. Firstly, many untrained or relatively little trained people
(for their specific work or in general) entered the factories; then,
the lengthening of the working day and, in not a few cases,
insufficient nourishment, pressed down productivity per hour and
even per lengthened working day; finally dissatisfaction with the
progress of the war, feelings of frustration in respect of the home
policy of the Government, etc., had a depressing effect on
productivity.

For one industry we have fairly reliable data on productivity:
namely the coal industry. The history of productivity in coal
mining is one of the most interesting because it reflects so many
aspects of the development of labour conditions during the present
and during the last war:*

PRODUCTIVITY IN COAL MINING PER WEEK, 1913–1918 AND
1938–1943

Year	Output per Worker and Week		Year	Output per Worker and Week	
	Tons	1913 = 100		Tons	1938 = 100
1913	5·02	100	1938	5·57	100
1914	Not available		1939	5·81	104
1915	5·21	104	1940	5·72	103
1916	5·03	100	1941	5·67	102
1917	4·79	95	1942	5·50	99
1918	4·45	89	1943	5·29	95

* Cf. Hansard, June 22, 1943, and *The Ministry of Labour Gazette*, May, 1944.

During the last war productivity at first showed no decline; on the contrary, it increased as the mass of the workers thought that the war was waged in their own interest and gave of their best. In the course of the war, production declined with increasing rapidity. This decline was due to a variety of causes: to declining health and stamina, to a deterioration of the working force from the point of view of age and skill, to a small extent to the working of poorer seams, to a small extent to technical difficulties of production (machinery, props, etc.), and finally to an ever increasing degree during the war, to the realization of the workers that that war was not a just war, not a war waged in the interests of the people.

How different has been the development during the present war. In spite of the demands upon the physical endurance of the miners whose average age has increased and whose health and physical strength has deteriorated during the course of the war, in spite of the growing technical difficulties which are worse to-day than in 1918, production remained above the 1938 level in 1940 and 1941, was about the same in 1938 and 1942, and began to decline below it only in 1943. It declined in 1943 partly because of the physical exhaustion of the miners, and because of technical and man-power difficulties (proportion of face workers!) and partly—this is the most serious part of it—because of a certain amount of frustration, falling for provocations of reactionaries, pro-fascists, etc., and similar causes, all connected with the growing dissatisfaction and cynicism in regard to the pursuit of the war and the home policy of the Government. Now, if this occurs during an unjust, imperialist war, it is only to be greeted as a sign of awakening of the class consciousness of the workers, of their growing awareness for the tasks which history has set them, of their leadership of the people towards a better future. But if it occurs in a just war against Fascism, this is a most serious sign for the success of the utter-reactionaries and for the relative failure of the progressive forces to rouse the people against the forces of reaction who from outside and to a small degree also from inside menace the present and the future of the people.

Although we have no figures available for industry as a whole or for other individual branches of the national war effort, I believe that the development in the coal industry during 1943 is by no means an isolated one, and can be found also in other industries—in some perhaps even more sharply expressed than in coal. I also believe that, in spite of a certain physical weariness, productivity would again go up, and probably reach unprecedented heights, if the military development were to show a turn in the strategy of Britain, a turn towards an all-out-effort to crush Fascism as quickly as possible, and if at the same time the home-policy of the Government were to indicate the resolution necessary to work out a future for the British people which they regard worthy of the greatest exertions to-day. *Such a turn in the course of events would mobilize an enormous amount of latent man-power, and would increase very considerably the labour force of the nation without an increase in the number of men and women at work.*

*   *   *

The combination of long hours of work and resulting fatigue, the employment of man-power which had not worked at all as wage earners before, the shifting of men and women from jobs in which they had worked for a long time to others with which they were not familiar, and the drive for greater intensity of work led during the last as well as during the present war to a not inconsiderable increase in accidents. No general accident rates are available for the last war, neither per 1,000 men employed nor per hour of exposure; there are not even any absolute figures on the total number of people injured. The only statistics at our disposal refer to fatal accidents, and these are usually statistics of absolute figures which do not give a clear picture of the real increase in accidents.

FATAL ACCIDENTS, 1914 TO 1918

Year	Factories and Workshops Total Number	Coal Mining per 1,000 employed	Other Mining per 1,000 employed	Quarrying	Railways Total Number
1914	1,287	1·15	1·01	1·20	477
1915	1,404	1·36	1·06	1·19	471
1916	1,507	1·32	1·18	1·20	453
1917	1,585	1·34	1·22	1·28	382
1918	1,579	1·39	0·91	1·55	337

Fatal accidents in factories and workshops rose constantly, most in 1915, less in 1916 and less again in 1917; in 1918 they declined slightly. But while the number of accidents rose that of the total number of employed declined or if it increased occasionally a little, it did not reach the pre-war level. The fatal accident rate in factories and workshops was even higher, therefore, during the last war as compared with 1914 than the above figures indicate. Fatal accidents in coal mining rose rapidly from 1914 to 1915, and remained through all the war years not inconsiderably above the 1914 level. For the railways no data are available to check upon the number of workers employed. In conclusion we can say that the fatal accident rate rose during the last war, and as far as we can measure it, it seems that the increase in the rate per 1,000 men employed of 15 to 20 per cent in coal mining is not an unusual one.

A highly interesting set of figures on fatal cases of certain industrial diseases can be put together on the basis of the report of the Chief Inspector of Factories for 1919 (p. 60):

DEATHS FROM CERTAIN INDUSTRIAL DISEASES, 1912 TO 1918

Year and Average	Lead Poisoning	Arsenic Poisoning	Toxic Jaundice	Anthrax	Total
1912–1914	33	—	—	7	40
1915–1917	21	2	34	12	69
1918	11	1	10	8	30

The table shows how physicians have become successful in dealing with lead poisoning, and how preventive or curative measures drove down the death rate from this disease. At the same time we observe how the production of new kinds of goods during the war—the effects of the use of tetrachlorethane when applied as a dope in the manufacture of aeroplanes in the case of toxic jaundice *—creates new industrial diseases and how, after an initial, often very rapid increase in the number of cases, medicine and preventive measures succeed in driving down the number and percentage of those affected or killed. But in spite of counter-measures the increase in the number of diseases was so great that the number of fatal cases rose very considerably during the first war years as compared with pre-war years.

* See Report of the Chief Inspector of Factories for 1917, pp. 18–20.

For the present war we have at our disposal vastly more material on the development of accidents. Although, for reasons of security, the Government does not publish any data on the rate of accidents, the figures given on their absolute number speak for themselves. The report of the Chief Inspector of Factories for 1942 gives the following figures on the number of accidents:

REPORTABLE ACCIDENTS, 1938 TO 1942

Year	Fatal Accidents	Variation on Previous Year	Non-Fatal Accidents	Variation on Previous Year
1938	944	—	179,159	—
1939	1,104	+ 17 per cent	192,371	+ 7 per cent
1940	1,372	+ 24 per cent	230,607	+ 20 per cent
1941	1,646	+ 20 per cent	269,652	+ 17 per cent
1942	1,363	— 17 per cent	313,267	+ 16 per cent

Accidents have risen enormously during the present war. True, employment has also slowly risen, and the number of hours worked have risen too—but these rises were small indeed as compared with the rise in the number of fatal accidents. Total accidents in the factories from 1938 to 1942 rose by 75 per cent. According to the above quoted estimate by Nicholson the total number of employed in factories as well as elsewhere in civilian jobs has increased by about 6 per cent between 1938 and 1942. This means that the total number of accidents per 1,000 employed has risen by two-thirds; and if we take into account Nicholson's estimate of the increase in the total number of hours worked, we arrive at an increase in the rate of accidents per hour of exposure of about 50 per cent. Even if Nicholson's figures are no more than ingenious estimates and refer not to exactly the same group of workers as the accident statistics, the result of better figures would not be much different from ours: the accident rate in industry per worker and per hour of work has increased in fact by about half in the course of the war—and it has increased from year to year, and though the increase was smaller in the last years of the war, it was still very high indeed.

But the Chief Inspector has not only prepared for us this highly important table. He has added to it another which gives us deeper insight in the development of accidents:

REPORTABLE ACCIDENTS, FATAL AND NON-FATAL, 1938 TO 1942

Year	Adult Males	Adult Females	Male Young Persons	Female Young Persons
1938	134,752	14,626	22,922	7,803
1939	146,417	17,029	22,364	7,665
1940	173,228	23,766	26,492	8,493
1941	191,343	42,857	27,757	9,341
1942	203,865	71,244	29,028	10,493

Percentage Increase of
1942 over 1938   51 per cent   389 per cent   27 per cent   34 per cent

Two columns are of special interest in this table : the development of accidents among adult men and among adult women. The accident rate among adult men per 1,000 employed has increased by about 50 per cent, as their number has probably changed only little. As to adult women : the number of accidents has increased between seven and eight times as much as that of men, and even if, because of the increase of the number of women employed, their rate of accidents has not risen quite as much, it was probably about 300 per cent above the 1938 level or four times as high. The enormous rise in the number of accidents among women confirms the fact that it is chiefly those who have freshly entered industry, or have done so after long unemployment, and those who have changed their jobs during the war in order to do more important work, who are especially susceptible to accidents. This does not apply equally to men and to women, because the women are doing work in this war which before, even in 1914–18, had been men's work only. To both of them applies a tendency among employers, especially during the first year of the war, to relax in safety measures.

If we regard the increased number of accidents as a sacrifice of civilian man-power for the war, we get the following number of losses :

INCREASED ACCIDENTS OVER THE 1938 LEVEL, 1939 TO 1942

Year	Adult Workers Men	Women	Juveniles
1939	11,665	3,403	696
1940	38,476	9,140	4,260
1941	56,591	28,231	6,373
1942	69,113	56,618	8,796
Total:	175,845	97,392	18,733

Those who explained that no soldiers must be "sacrificed" for the Second Front before "sufficient metal" were available, should ponder these figures, should ponder, how millions were sent into the industrial battle, how within four years of war the number of wounded on the industrial front was not far from half a million, more than two-fifth of them women and juveniles.

While it is not possible to compare the rate of increase of accidents in the two wars, it is obvious that the experiences of the last war have not contributed to lower materially the rate of increase during the present one. On the contrary, I would not be surprised if a detailed investigation of the basis of unpublished material would show for the last war a rate of accidents very similar or possibly even relatively lower than during the present one. This does probably not hold true for industrial diseases for which, although no comparable figures have been published, I would not be surprised to find a relative improvement during the present as compared with the last war.

But one fact is definitely very different in the present and the last war: the relation between casualties among the workers who have joined the army and those who are working in industry on the home front has materially changed in favour of those in the army. The casualties on the home front as compared with those on the combat front have increased very considerably, indeed.

4. THE HEALTH OF THE WORKERS

There is prevalent in this country a dangerous illusion that the state of health of the people, while perhaps not as satisfactory as could be wished, is better than in pre-war years. The Press spreads the idea that the people of this country, and especially the workers, are surprisingly healthy, not only as compared with pessimistic expectations at the beginning of the war, but also as compared with the years before the war.

Let us first study the death rate from certain illnesses during the present and the last war:*

* Ministry of Health, Annual Report of the Chief Medical Officer, 1919–1920; Summary Report of the Ministry of Health for the period from April 1, 1941, to March 31, 1942, and for the year ended March 31, 1943.

DEATH RATES PER THOUSAND OF THE POPULATION

1914 TO 1918 AND 1939 TO 1942

Year	Cerebro-Spinal Fever	Diphtheria	Influenza	Measles	Scarlet Fever	Tuberculosis
1914	0·005	0·158	0·161	0·247	0·077	1·361
1939	0·012	0·051	0·193	0·007	0·004	0·618
1915	0·039	0·165	0·293	0·462	0·066	1·515
1940	0·062	0·060	0·277	0·021	0·004	0·679
1916	0·022	0·154	0·252	0·155	0·039	1·529
1941	0·052	0·064	0·166	0·028	0·004	0·691
1917	0·027	0·132	0·213	0·308	0·022	1·624
1942	0·029	0·044	0·082	0·011	0·003	0·616
1918	0·015	0·142	3·129	0·289	0·029	1·694

If we compare the figures for the years of the present and those for the last war we notice the considerable progress which medicine has made in the preservation of life. The death rate of such diseases as diphtheria, measles, scarlet fever and tuberculosis has gone down very considerably. But as during the last war so we notice during the present one a general tendency for deaths from such diseases to increase. Yet during the present war this increase stopped for many illnesses already in 1941, and among these six illnesses only two—cerebro-spinal fever and measles—show for 1942 a higher death rate than for 1939. Even tuberculosis shows a lower death rate in 1942 than in 1939! During the last war the death rate in 1917 was higher than that of 1914 in all but two cases (diphtheria and scarlet fever). Consequently, we are justified in saying that health or rather the death conditions in respect of these dangerous infectious diseases, while in the pattern of their development not fundamentally different as compared with the last war, are not inconsiderably better during the present one.

But these diseases and the deaths resulting from them are only a very small and minor aspect of the history of health conditions during the war. Of vastly more importance than these death statistics in the general story of the state of health of the people, is the story of what the Ministry of Health calls "positive health" in contrast to death statistics and to the incidence of infectious diseases. How has the general state of health of the people developed during the present war? Unfortunately we have no statistical data at our disposal. But this is the fault not of the state of statistical science but of the reluctance of the Ministry of Health to undertake the necessary investigations. If it says in its report for the year ending March 31, 1943: "There is in fact no simple way of measuring the health (in a positive sense) of 40,000,000 people, though existing methods are constantly being extended," then it is wrong. Of course, there are simple ways of measuring the state of health, one of them was tried out most successfully in the U.S.A. health survey of 1935–36.

But even without such a survey we can say that health conditions were surprisingly good during the first year or two of the war, as compared with what the authorities expected and as compared with pre-war years. What is the reason for this? The reason is a very simple one. Before the war there were about two million unemployed, many short-time workers, and others receiving an extremely low wage and living far below a standard guaranteeing decent health conditions. With the war unemployment began to disappear, so did short time, and at least some of the lowest paid groups of workers received not only absolute, but also real wage increases. That is, war brought a standard of living for millions of workers which peace did not guarantee them, and thus naturally led to an improvement in the nation's health. But in the course of time, that is, during the third and fourth year of war the beneficial effects began to be less felt. New factors of importance, such as the continued strain upon the physique of the worker, resulting from long working hours, considerable intensity of work, and so on, began to counterbalance and after some time to outweigh these improvements. *
The last report of the Ministry of Health, covering the year ending March 31, 1943, says: "Sample enquiries among doctors, considered in conjunction with the rising claims to sickness benefit under the National Health Insurance Scheme, suggest that there

---

* While the improvement in factory welfare facilities must be mentioned also among the beneficial factors, I believe that a more extended institution of such facilities could have postponed the deterioration of health conditions which we are experiencing in recent years.

was a considerable increase in short-term sickness during the year . . . an increase in minor illnesses might well be expected after more than three years of war with all its anxieties; long hours of employment, often on heavy and unusual work; shopping, travelling and housing difficulties; Civil Defence or Home Guard Duties; lack of holidays, and the black-out. There is no indication of an increase in long-term illness."

This is a very clear statement, and shows the general development of the state of health of the Nation. It shows that there is a deterioration, and it shows, that a further, more serious deterioration is to be expected—although the official report is careful in not pointing out this logical consequence. For it is obvious that the period since March, 1943, and that the future immediately before us, gives no reason to expect a lowering of the influence of the above mentioned factors upon the state of health of the people. Hours of work may have become somewhat shorter perhaps in a number of cases, but the general strain upon the health of the people, even if its pressure is not higher, has increased merely by its continuance. A constant strain leads not to a constant susceptibility to illness, but to an increasing one. And that is what happens to-day. But even more is happening. A constant increase in short-term and minor illnesses leads not only to a general weakening of the body and to increased susseptibility to minor and short-term illnesses, but prepares the way for an increase in long-term and major illnesses. There is, therefore, not the slightest reason for any optimism about the future development of health conditions among the workers. On the contrary, *if the war lasts much longer through procrastination in the military field, and if the armistice will not at the same time inaugurate a period of well-planned reconstruction, and if some work in this direction is not at once undertaken, we must reckon on a serious deterioration in the general state of health of the Nation, with possibly large scale epidemics of a very serious character.*

There is not the slightest reason for complacency, therefore, and if we do not watch out, the experience of the last war, when in 1918 the number of deaths from influenza increased so rapidly as to drive up not inconsiderably the general death rate, may be repeated in some form or other. *A combination of military aggressiveness and intelligent post-war planning will not only save ten thousands of British lives on the battlefield but hundred thousands of lives at home, endangered to-day by the strain of war.*

5. THE LABOUR MOVEMENT

As during the last war, so during the present war the Labour Movement has been officially recognized as an important element in the furtherance of a successful prosecution of the war. Leaders of the Trade Unions and of the Labour Party have been consulted and have been given positions of responsibility. As during the last war, members of the Labour Movement have become ministers, and thousands of Labour officials have been nominated to hundreds of committees.

But there is one, and absolutely decisive, difference between the position of Labour during the last and during the present war. The last war did not correspond to the interests of the working class. The Labour leaders in 1914–1918, who put themselves at the disposal of the Government, misled Labour, consciously or unconsciously. At first, the workers did not realize this; there were only a few who rebelled against the prosecution of the war, few who saw clearly the mistake which the majority of the Labour leadership committed. But in the course of time, war, the hardest teacher of all, pressed home to more and more workers the fact that they were being misled, against their own interests, to fight for the interests of capitalism. This growing clarity among the workers becomes very obvious from a study of the development of strikes. *

STRIKES AND LOCK-OUTS, 1914–1918

Year	Number of Strikers	Duration of Strikes (Workdays)
1914	447,000	9,878,000
1915	448,000	2,953,000
1916	276,000	2,446,000
1917	872,000	5,647,000
1918	1,116,000	5,875,000

Until 1916 the strike activity goes down or remains on a very low level; the first quarter of 1917 is still one of the lowest war strike quarters on record. But with the second quarter the strike

* *Abstract of Labour Statistics, 1927.*

activity begins to increase rapidly and continues, under fluctuations, to rise right into the first years of the peace. The workers had begun to realize where their true interests lay—although they let themselves be misled again, with the consequent failures of twenty years of war-breeding peace.

During the present war the situation is an altogether different one. True, this war is due to the weakness of the working class everywhere, except in the Soviet Union, during the years from 1918 to 1939, and to the policy of the ruling class of monopoly capitalists in the years of so-called peace. But it is equally true that the war against Fascism to-day is in the interest of the people, that its energetic persecution is the only way to make up for the weaknesses shown and for the mistakes made in the past years. To-day, there is a real unity of interest of all classes. To-day the leaders of Labour and the Trade Union officials who join the war effort, who are nominated to committees, and who enter the Government can from their place of activity further the interests of the people. For the present war is a just war, a war in the interest of us all, a war in which everybody must join and give of his best.

How, under such circumstances, has strike activity developed? Has it been lower than during the last war? Has it shown a tendency to decline instead of increasing as it did during the last war?

STRIKES AND LOCK-OUTS, 1939 TO 1943*

Year	Number of Strikers	Duration of Strikes (Workdays)
1939	337,000	1,360,000
1940	299,000	940,000
1941	360,000	1,080,000
1942	457,000	1,530,000
1943	557,000	1,810,000

The pattern of development is the same in this war as during the last war, although the character of the war is so vastly different. During the first year or two of the war strike activity declined. And then it continued to increase from year to year— the same in the unjust and in the just war. But this similarity is

* *The Ministry of Labour Gazette,* January, 1944.

only a superficial one. The real difference becomes obvious when
we compare the absolute amount of workdays struck:

WORKDAYS STRUCK IN TWO WARS

Year	Workdays	Year	Workdays
1914	9,878,000	1917	5,647,000
1939	1,360,000	1942	1,530,000
1915	2,953,000	1918	5,875,000
1940	940,000	1943	1,810,000
1916	2,446,000		
1941	1,080,000		

The strike level before the war of 1914–18 was a higher one
than that before the present war. During the first full year of war
strike activity declined, by more than two-thirds in 1915, and
by about a quarter in 1940. Between 1915 and 1917 strike
activity rose by about 100 per cent; between 1940 and 1942
strike activity, although on an extremely low level in 1940, rose
only by about 50 per cent. And although it rose again from 1942
to 1943, it remained very much below the 1918 level. But even
these figures do not show the whole difference between the two
wars. For during the last war there were a considerable number
of very large scale strikes, beginning in the second half of 1915
with the strike of the South Wales miners, comprising 200,000
workers. During this war, however, there was up to 1943 no single
large scale strike comprising 50,000 or more workers; and that
is the decisive difference For it is extremely unlikely to have even
during the most just of wars a clean strike record in a capitalist
country. For there will always be employers who will provoke
strikes, and there will always be elements within the working
class who are interested in misleading the workers. It would
simply be closing one's eyes to the realities of the situation to ask
for a clean strike record in a just war under conditions of monopoly capitalism. But this does not mean that the number of days
struck during a just war must increase as it has done during the
last three years. That clearly is a reflection of a certain weakness
of the progressive forces. It is no reflection upon the ruling class
—for those who expect the monopoly capitalists, even if for their
own reasons they join the just cause, to give up completely their
fight on the home front have not taken their measure, have not

understood the working of the class struggle. And those who do not draw the consequences of this situation show that they do not realize the full task before the working class in this just war. The increase in strike activity during the last two years is clearly due to an increasing aggressiveness of the monopoly capitalists. And they have dared to become more aggressive again because, on the one hand, they believe that victory is a certainty, and therefore, they want to prepare for peace by taking away to-day many of the war-time gains of labour—and because, on the other hand, the progressive forces and their representatives in the Government have not pressed the interests of the progressive cause sufficiently.

The strike record of Britain during the last few years shows that the people realize the true character of this war, that they do not put first minor specific interests of the working class, that they can distinguish between the fight against the chief cause of reaction, German Fascism, and the fight for certain palliatives against the evils of capitalism in their own country. But it also shows that Labour must lose ground, if it does not take up a more determined attitude against those monopoly capitalists who want to use the war against Fascism as a cover for a war against Labour. Only if British Labour knows how to fight these elements to-day will the people of this country be victorious in this war as well as in the peace following it. That is the lesson to be drawn from these strike statistics, a lesson taught to the observant progressive in so many fields of activity to-day—on the battlefront as well as at home.

And some of the pre-requisites for this march of Labour, leading the people to a future worthwhile fighting for, have developed very well during the last few years. One of the most important of them is the growth of the organization of Labour. True, the Labour Party has declined in membership from 2,663,067 members in 1939 to 2,453,392 members in 1942, while during the last war it increased from 1,612,147 in 1914 to 3,013,129 members in 1918. But the trade unions have grown rapidly from 6,231,000 members in 1939 to 7,781,000 in 1942—which can be compared with a growth from 4,145,000 in 1914 to 6,533,000 in 1918. And the Communist Party which was small in 1939 has grown into a mass party. When the present urgent drive to increase the politico-organizational consciousness of the trade union members has succeeded, when the political levy is being paid by a rapidly increasing number of trade unionists, when the Labour Party begins to grow again, and a strong Communist Party is affiliated to it, then we can say that such an organization of Labour furnishes a solid basis for the fight for progress and against reaction and the interests vested in the poverty and misery of the people.

INDEX

I.—INDEX OF TABLES

II.—INDEX OF NAMES

(PERSONS, PLACES, PEOPLES)

III.—GENERAL INDEX